NO, YOU CANNOT
JUST SNAP OUT OF IT!

*A Memoir for People Dealing with Depression and
Anxiety that Extend Beyond Mere Thoughts*

EVELYN S. RODAS

EVELYN S. RODAS

Printed Worldwide
First Printing 2023
First Edition 2023

10 9 8 7 6 5 4 3 2 1

e-book ASIN B0CCMYQ832
ISBN 979-8-9872068-1-2
Paperback ISBN 979-8-9872068-0-5
Hardcover ISBN 979-8-9872068-2-9

doubledolphinpublishing@writeme.com
www.doubledolphinpublishing.com

Disclaimer

The author has no affiliations or financial involvement that conflicts with the material presented in this book. She does not represent any individual, company, corporation, or brand. The views expressed herein are solely those of the author.
All the events in this memoir are true to the best of the author's present recollection. Names, places, and circumstances may have been changed to protect the identity of certain parties.
This book is for informational purposes only. It is not a substitute for professional medical advice or treatment. Consult with your physician for this purpose.
Although the author has tried to keep the information in this book as accurate and timely as possible, neither she nor the publisher can accept legal responsibility for any error or omission.

NO, YOU CANNOT
JUST SNAP OUT OF IT!

https://www.amazon.com/Cannot-Dealing-Depression-Anxiety-Thoughts-ebook/dp/B0CCMYQ832/ref=monarch_sidesheets

ABOUT THE AUTHOR

Evelyn S. Rodas is an author with a mission to raise awareness about the need to break with old paradigms about major depressive disorder, anxiety, and mental illness and explore other concepts more in tune with their real meaning.

Through almost three decades of fighting unipolar depression, **Evelyn** has gained one-of-a-kind subjective experiences and crucial knowledge on the disease, which provides her with vital elements to describe clinical depression in an authentic and unique way. By doing so, she intends to bring hope to anyone struggling with this disease and feels no solution exists. She wants you to know that she once felt like that but came out triumphant in the end.

Evelyn S. Rodas points out that if she had known the vast information she now possesses about depression and anxiety, much of her suffering could have been avoided. For this reason, she aims to provide other patients with a shortcut to fully understand their condition's possible root causes so they will not have to struggle for years before they find effective solutions.

DEDICATION

This book is dedicated to the victims of misinformation and wrong beliefs that surround major depression, anxiety, and mental illness in general.

"Like the fragile dove on the cover of this book, your wings have broken, and your feet are tied.

The other birds cheer you up, inviting you to come along, fly with them, and have a jolly time.

The truth is that your wounds are invisible to the eyes of those who see you from up high."

READER DISCRETION IS ADVISED

This book contains explicit language related to serious human struggles, major suffering, and suicide. If you are feeling sensitive or emotional at this moment, please choose another time to read this content.

TABLE OF CONTENTS

INTRODUCTION

Is depression real, or is it only in the mind?

Is it a disease of the soul?

Is it true that everybody gets it sooner or later?

At what point does a depressed mood become an illness?

Should I see a psychologist or a psychiatrist?

Should I take medicine or not?

Is depression heritable?

How do I know if I have depression?

Why do some get depressed after trauma while others do not?

Is it really the evilest existence?

In this book, you will learn about possible reasons preventing your recovery if you are struggling with major depression and do not seem to be getting better. You will find answers to the above questions and much more. This book offers a revolutionary way to conceptualize DEPRESSION, ANXIETY, AND MENTAL ILLNESS, drawing a clear picture of what they are and leaving aside what they are commonly believed to be.

Several years ago, as I began to hunt for and collect information about major depression, I ran into a lot of conflicting arguments, misconceptions, misbeliefs, disbeliefs, biases, you name it. All these factors have contributed to people interpreting depression in a variety of ways. Nowadays, the word "depression" can mean so many different things to different people, from sadness, disappointment, grief, pessimism, and fear to low self-esteem, lack of motivation, lack of willpower, anger, insecurity, and even laziness.

For several years I have wanted to do something to stop the incredibly large amount of speculation that could not be more detached from reality. And most importantly, I want to help people become aware that...

"Not all depressions are created equal!"

I have come to the realization that there is a big need for a more effective approach to address this topic. An approach that will facilitate the understanding that the depression most people know about has almost nothing to do with the disease very few have heard of.

At present, not having clear boundaries between psychology and psychiatry is a serious issue. This lack of clarity is misguiding people to talk about complex biological disorders as if they were only psychological or environmental issues.

I know depression as a disease. I live with it, and I go to bed with it. I have known it for almost *three decades*! I have priceless, authentic, firsthand experiences I wish to share so more people can learn about the facts surrounding this ravaging malady. My goal is to show clinical depression from a different angle, from the inside out, which is the only way we can aim to describe it authentically.

I am convinced that if most of us get an accurate understanding of what this illness is about, we will be able to help our loved ones or ourselves more promptly and effectively. By learning the right information and getting the appropriate tools, we may be able to prevent, conquer, and even maintain the sickness out of our lives. I am determined to put all the knowledge I have gained about depression through all these years at the service of the victims of this pervasive disease. Maybe you, who are reading this book, are looking for guidance and moral support from someone you can identify with. Someone who knows how savage this disease can be and understands what you are going through. Someone who has walked in your shoes before, someone who can reassure you that it is possible, based on my own experience, to conquer this major disease. I want to be that someone.

According to the World Health Organization, around 280 million people suffer from depression worldwide. We must agree that a public health issue of this magnitude should call for massive actions from health authorities and the scientific community. So many millions of people would benefit from the development of evidence-based methods of diagnosing unipolar depression and other so-called mental disorders. They would also benefit from the development of innovative medical treatments that would ideally cause fewer negative side effects than some of the current ones. More importantly, many lives could be saved if more advanced measures were implemented.

To demonstrate how significant the lack of accurate information on depression is, I am presenting a compilation of several conversations and exchanges from people in chat rooms on depression. Here, they have candidly expressed their own unique concepts of depression:

1.- "Keep on trucking, trying to make everyone have the exact same cookie cutter biochemistry. These variations in chemical imbalances are the defining blueprints of a personality, not a sign of abnormality. What exactly is abnormal? Who decides what normal is? The majority?"

2.- "I have often said that if every counseling patient won a big lottery right before entering a counseling session, 90 percent would have their immediate problems relieved, most of their sadness lifted. Money doesn't solve every problem, but it does relieve a lot of burdens preoccupying a lot of Americans today."

3.- "I honestly feel as though people are depressed because they live in a depressing world. If anything, people who are generally happy are some of the most seriously ill."

4.- "I see the DIFFERENCE between SADNESS and DEPRESSION as: 1st is an EMOTION, and 2nd is TRYING TO HIDE that emotion..."

5.- "Pretty sure there is an overwhelming correlation between income inequality and these higher rates of depression. I am surprised the number of people called depressed isn't bigger. What are the numbers? 80 percent of Westerners don't even have $1000 in the bank."

6.- "There is a large majority of people who either don't realize or are willfully ignorant of the fact that they will never be able to retire, let alone comfortably. Or maybe they do realize this, which is why they are eating/drinking/medicating themselves to death."

7.- "I have been told by a trustworthy person that depression and anxiety can be the result of a spirit."

8.- "You only really know what depression is when you've experienced it, or at least that's my experience... So, I guess you are better able to tell the difference if you've had it, too. I will never use the word 'depressed' so lightly since having it anyway."

9.- "Depression, like so many mental illnesses, is not mathematics; it just doesn't work that way. Otherwise, it would be very simple to solve everything with just one treatment. I think it's perfectly fine that you've found your answer and it works for you. I don't dismiss theories, thoughts, or opinions just because they differ from mine. Some people get better when involved in a religion, a hobby, or alternative approaches. I believe in whatever works."

10.- "It is unfortunate that people ill with depression are told that everything is in their head, which only makes them feel worse."

Throughout this book, I will demonstrate that except for the last three statements, all the other opinions are based on bias and ignorance, unfortunately.

To my readers who are currently fighting this disease called depression, I want you to know I am aware of the almost indescribable misery major depression and anxiety are causing you. I know how isolating it feels to see everybody around you breathe freely, smoothly, without minimal effort while you are gasping for every single breath you take. I have written this book with you in mind.

CHAPTER 1

DESTINY, CHANCE, FATE. WHAT'S LIFE ABOUT?

One summer morning in the early nineties, the light of dawn seeped into my bedroom. A gentle breeze also drifted in through the open window, carrying with it the melodic exchanges of birdsong. Their singing and the smell of that gentle breeze transported me back to the worry-free beach days of my childhood when, together with my siblings, I ran merrily along the shore, experiencing the pleasurable sensation of my feet touching warm sand.

Far from comforting me, these happy memories made me feel homesick. Adverse circumstances I will talk about later forced me into leaving home to stay in this place where I had to share spaces with other people, at least temporarily. Anyway, the day had dawned crisp and clear, so I decided to embrace the hope that it would be a rather uplifting one. This good weather suggested it was going to be a better day for me. Nothing indicated I should prepare for what was about to happen.

I got out of bed and tried to take a shower when I realized there was no hot water. I cannot stand showering in cold water, so it seemed like not showering at all was the only choice I had. I was about to change into my clothes for the day when it dawned on me that I could shower in the next room. I asked for permission and got lucky with a positive answer. At least, I thought I was lucky.

I took a hot shower, feeling very pleased. Upon finishing, I wrapped myself in my big white towel, came out, and headed to my room. As I was walking out, I heard a shrill voice behind my back. She sounded enraged. When I turned around, I saw an older woman standing by the window, eyes wide and red, like fire. Her body posture showed she was agitated. She was yelling and screaming insults. I soon realized the insults were meant for me. I froze for a moment, trying to understand what was happening. Suddenly, she charged toward me. I held the towel tightly around my body and hurried to my room. I could feel her following me. I rushed into my room and locked the door behind me. Immediately after, I let my body fall onto the bed. My heart was pounding, and it felt like it was about to jump out of my chest. I stayed there for quite some time, trying to regain my composure.

This incident pulled me back to reality. A cruel reality I had been trying not to think of since I'd wound up here. My eyes moved from the dull white walls to the nurse's button beside my bed, to the plastic pitcher of water … and came to rest on the chart at the end of the bed listing my psych meds.

I had never in my life thought of the possibility of ending up in a psych ward. I guess most people wouldn't think of the possibility, either. I had always heard this kind of place was for "mental" patients, or what is colloquially called "crazy." I had been diagnosed with major depressive disorder, but I was certainly not crazy. Nonetheless, since MDD is listed as a mental illness, it automatically makes me a mentally ill person. You may be thinking it doesn't make any sense. Let me tell you, when it comes to mental illness, a lot of things don't make much sense. You will learn about this as you continue reading.

THE MANIFESTATION OF THE NIGHTMARE

By telling my story, I intend to go beyond the theories of how MDD feels to the actual experience of living through a serious case of the disease. Believe me; there's a whole world that separates them. First, I would like to tell you about how I got to the psych clinic. I am going to start with the day that marked the beginning of the nightmare.

It was morning, and I was giving a class to a group of children as part of my school training. In those moments, I felt physically and emotionally exhausted, like a car that had consumed every single drop of gas from its tank. I didn't feel I could continue moving. If I could, I would have lain down on the floor to rest.

Upon finishing my class, I went to the bathroom. I got my face wet and put cold water on my head. But I didn't feel better.

Instead, I was on the brink of collapse. A bitter cry came from deep inside me. Realizing I no longer had any control over my emotions made me feel so much anguish. I worried someone would see me in that state. What would they think of a young adult girl who cried uncontrollably? I needed to calm down before someone knocked on that bathroom door. But how to do it if I couldn't appease myself? I stayed in there for several minutes until I managed to draw strength from somewhere and forced myself to act as if everything was fine.

I was supposed to go back to my office work, but I realized I couldn't keep going feeling like this, so I went home instead.

My mom was surprised to see me back early.

"Evelyn, why are you back so early? Did anything happen?"

"No, Mom. I just came back home because I wasn't feeling well."

"Your stomach again?"

"No, it's not my stomach this time."

"So, what's wrong with you, darling?"

"I'm not sure. I don't know exactly what it is. I have been feeling very tired these days, and it stresses me because I can't do a good job."

"How exactly do you feel now?"

"I feel nervous, stressed out, my muscles are tense, and I just feel beyond exhausted. All I want to do is relax, but no matter how hard I try, I just can't feel at ease."

"How long have you been feeling like that?"

"Long ago. But it wasn't this bad. It's been getting worse as months go by."

"Why didn't you tell me before?"

"I thought I was just tired, and it would go away if I dedicated time to rest. But I just can't feel rested!

Mom gave me a sleeping pill she herself took at nighttime. It made me sleep for a few hours. When I woke up, I felt just as bad. Again, I started living my internal struggle to free myself from that physical tension and the emotional anguish stuck in my chest.

It was evening already; I was lying in bed in a fetal position. I heard people talking in the living room and recognized a voice. It was Mayra, one of my sisters, talking with friends. I wasn't following their conversation. I was not interested, but I could hear the noise they were making, which was bothering me. I felt the volume of their voices began to rise gradually. Each time, the noise felt closer to my ears. It became so disturbing I felt like covering my ears tightly with my hands. But I could still hear the loudness. I tried putting more and more pressure on my ears, but it didn't help. I took a pillow and put it around my head, but that didn't help either. Then, I added another pillow. Same thing. Their voices boomed like powerful speakers right next to my ears. It seemed all the noises around me managed to penetrate any barriers. The volume kept increasing, and it began to hurt. It started feeling like the noise was drilling into my eardrums.

In my despair, I jumped out of bed and ran to the backyard, trying to flee from that torment. I sat on the floor and leaned against the wall for support. My heart was racing, my body was rigid, and I was having difficulty breathing.

My mom came over right away. She saw me on the ground, completely defenseless, like a dying dog, panting in agony.

"Oh, my God! Sweetie, what happened? What is going on?"

I couldn't even answer. It felt like I was being strangled, and I was fighting with all my might, trying to free myself.

Mom got desperate and started screaming for help: "Mayra! Rosie! Yuri! Go find your brother Walter. Tell him to go get a taxi. Evelyn has got really bad. We must take her to the hospital. Hurry up!"

At the ER, they gave me a shot of tranquilizers, and it made me sleep. The following morning, I saw the psychiatrist. She asked me several questions about myself and my lifestyle. She told me she thought I was stressed out and that I needed to slow down. She prescribed some medication and told me I had to take it for seven days straight. She emphasized that I must stay home and sleep. She prohibited me from going places or visiting anybody; I had to take the medicine and rest exclusively.

I took the medicine and rested for the first three days. After that, I was feeling better, and now that sense of total despair was gone. I felt good enough not to stay in bed. Not obeying the doctor's recommendations, I got up and started cleaning my house. I kept doing all kinds of house chores instead of resting. The problem with me was that I couldn't fail at doing something if I felt I could do it.

The relief was palpable on the following day, so I got up and went back to work. The energy I had recovered allowed me to continue doing what was really important to me: being able to go back to work and school. I threw away the medication because I felt I didn't need it anymore.

The next weekend, I was at home having breakfast. I remember spreading creamy avocado on a piece of bread. I have always loved avocados. Man, that food tasted so good; I was enjoying every single bite. In the middle of this delightful experience, I felt like the top of my brain was pulled down like a lever pulled violently. Almost instantly, I lost all strength in my body. I felt like a puppet when they cut the strings off. I hunched back and started shivering. Deeply disturbing emotions took over my whole being. Immediately after, my body started to reject the food I was eating. In the blink of an eye, I was uninterested. Then, I even disliked it, and a little after that, I could no longer stand it. The rejection went to such an extent that I couldn't even swallow the food I already had in my mouth. I spit it out, using my fingers to remove it faster.

My family rushed me back to the ER for a second time. Once there, like on the previous occasion, they gave me a shot of a tranquilizer. I slept through the night, and the next morning, I got to see the psychiatrist again, the same one I had seen previously. I was sincere with her. I told her I had taken the medication only three days instead of seven, as she had prescribed, and I hadn't really dedicated the time to rest during that week. I went back to work instead.

The doctor reprimanded me for not having followed her instructions. She commented that my problem seemed more complex, and so I would need to get serious and compromise to do as I was told. The diagnosis this time was major depressive disorder.

At this point, I understood my health issue wasn't simple, and it would need some time to resolve. I also reflected on all the trouble I had been causing my family. I wondered whether they would need to bring me to the ER again. I thought maybe it would be better to stay at the hospital so Mom wouldn't need to bring me back once more. Also, staying there would make me comply with the treatment time the doctor had recommended."

KEY QUESTIONS THAT NEED CLEAR ANSWERS

1.- Is mental illness a "real" illness?

Some people believe mental illness is not real and illnesses that fall under this umbrella are made up. They say mental illness of any kind is a complete lie created by special interests. The argument is that the pharmaceutical industry wants to convince more and more people that they have an illness of this nature so they can make extensive profits from the sale of their psychotropic medications. Logically, the more people diagnosed with mental illness, the more consumption of medication, and the more money they can make.

This theory could explain why the number of diagnosable mental disorders has been steadily on the rise for several decades (from 106 disorders in 1952 to 180 in 1968, to 265 in 1980, to 365 in 1994, to 400 + disorders listed in the 2013 DSM-V).

Others have suggested that some individuals pretend to have a mental illness because they want attention, or they prefer to blame their made-up illness for their failures, because they are lazy and don't want to go to work, or simply because they want to take some time off.

This argument could explain why mental illness (depression) is the leading cause of disability around the world.

On the other hand, people who do, in fact, suffer from mental illness become outraged when they hear these rude and dismissive comments. They feel offended when critics disrespect their suffering and minimize the seriousness of their disease. Moreover, people suffering from major depressive disorder (MDD) who received treatment with antidepressants and got better, as a result, have disproven the argument that states, "There is no evidence that medication works" because it did work for them. If it hadn't been for the medicines, they wouldn't be alive.

2.- Is major depressive disorder (MDD) a disease of the soul?

Many people believe human beings have a soul. Others don't believe we have one. Consequently, the definition of the soul can vary, depending on each individual. The definition of disease, however, is very clear. A disease affects an organism's body, organs, tissues, or cells.

If we have a soul, it certainly isn't made out of matter. Therefore, there's no such thing as diseases of the soul or spirit.

3.- How is MDD diagnosed?

In Psychiatry, unlike other branches of medicine, doctors don't have quantitative medical tests at their disposal to assist them with the diagnosing process when it comes to mental illness. They can't do blood tests, X-rays, or a urinalysis. Nor can they culture microorganisms. Consequently, psychiatrists are not required to provide conclusive evidence to back up their diagnoses; they are just expected to follow the standard criteria listed in the DSM-5. The diagnoses are mainly based on interviews, symptoms, and observation.

However, we need to acknowledge that the process of diagnosing an illness based on symptoms can sometimes be fallible. One of the issues with this model of diagnosis is the fact that two people can show the same symptoms but for different reasons, just like two people can show different symptoms for the same reason.

Some people have argued that psychiatric diagnoses are not as objective as their physiological counterparts but are rather more like opinions and, therefore, subject to implicit biases even when propounded by competent psychiatrists or psychologists.

Let's consider the case of homosexuality. For many years, homosexuality was listed as a mental illness in the Diagnostic and Statistical Manual. In 1974, the American Psychiatric

Association removed the diagnosis of homosexuality from the DSM-2.

I have seen some people share their anecdotes about the time when they were diagnosed with a mental illness. Some talked about getting two different diagnoses from two different doctors. Others stated they were given two or even three different diagnoses at different times by the same doctor.

These examples lead us to the realization that even when we get diagnosed with an illness of this nature, it doesn't always mean we totally, conclusively, and undeniably have the illness.

4.- Should I take medication or just talk therapy?

Many disciplines are involved in studying, researching, and treating major depression and anxiety, which is good. Nonetheless, this can also turn out to be very confusing because we don't always know exactly what each professional can do for us. (Medical and non-medical). People wonder who they should see first and why.

Below are listed some of the various disciplines and professionals around anxiety, depression, and mental illness in general:

1.- Psychiatry

2.- Neurology

3.- Neuropsychiatry

4.- Psychology

5.- Neuropsychology

6.- Clinical Psychology

7.- Psychotherapy

8.- Psychoanalysis

9.- *Counseling*
10.- *Social Worker*
11.- *Psychiatric Nurse*
12.- *Any Medical Doctor whose specialty is not Psychiatry*
(We don't need to see a psychiatrist exclusively to be prescribed psychiatric medication. I wonder why. Would it be okay for a heart surgeon to operate on brains?)
13.- *Mental Health Professionals (It's not clear who else is included in this category).*

Case Study

Jenny was a hardworking woman, the mother of a little girl whom she adored. Her boyfriend and the father of her daughter bordered on being lazy and unmotivated. Jenny was hopeful he would soon become responsible and start helping more.

Time passed by, but the boyfriend still wasn't helping much. One day, they had a serious argument and broke up. He left home. Jenny was convinced it was the right thing to do, although she was hoping he would change and decide to become a better father and partner. In the back of her mind, Jenny envisioned her daughter growing up with both parents.

After some time, she heard some gossip. Jenny's boyfriend was living with a close friend of hers. This caught Jenny by surprise. She froze! After all, they had been together for quite some time, and he was still her child's father. But now he was in a relationship with her friend. That seemed too much to handle. Jenny felt devastated.

A few weeks passed, and Jenny fell into a depression, as most people would call it. Her family got worried and advised her to see a doctor.

After talking to Jenny for a few minutes, the doctor diagnosed her with depression and proceeded to prescribe medication.

Jenny was surprised by what the doctor had just told her. Back home, she decided not to take the antidepressant medication. She made the decision to become better on her own because she felt it was under her control. Sometime later, Jenny began to feel normal again.

Maybe we should try to answer this question: Was Jenny suffering from a disease, or was she having a reactive emotional crisis?

These are the typical stages most of us go through when facing an unfortunate event: First, we feel devastated. Then, we fall into a depressed mood (the time we stay in this stage varies depending on the seriousness of the event and the person's temperament). If there's no physical impediment, the next stage is recovery.

In a situation like Jenny's, when the affected person feels he/she can help themselves, they can go ahead and find their own resources to tame their emotions, as Jenny did.

On the other hand, if we feel we need emotional support, we can talk to anybody we trust and feel can help us, like family members, close friends, the clergy, etc.

Finally, if we feel the situation is overwhelming or almost out of our control, it is advisable to seek professional assistance.

I should say there was a tragic side to a story like Jenny's. Because she was told she had this major disease, she will always believe she did have it. Because she was apparently able to beat it all by herself, without medication, she may become judgmental of people who can't bounce back on their own due to physical impediments. She may, in good faith, advise ill people not to take the medical treatment they actually need. This is the way misconceptions regarding MDD are created.

5.- What is the difference between a psychologist and a psychiatrist?

When talking about these two professionals, we usually think of them as the same without making any distinction. We commonly hear things like this: "She should go see a psychologist or a psychiatrist." Or "He should look for a psychological or psychiatric treatment."

It is crucial that we know the difference between **a psychologist and a psychiatrist** before we start looking for a good fit for us.

Psychiatrists attend medical school and become doctors (M.D. or D.O.) before undergoing specialist training in mental health. Because they are physicians, they are licensed to prescribe medications. Psychiatrists tend to treat complex and severe mental illnesses, the ones believed to have organic roots.

Because psychiatrists study psychology too, they understand the links between mental and physical problems. Psychiatrists can provide a wide range of treatments, from verbal-based psycho-therapy to general medical care, including checking your physical health.

A **Psychologist** is a practitioner who studies behavior and the way in which the mind works. They aren't physicians, and for that reason, they can't write prescriptions. Psychologists tend to treat conditions that are not believed to have organic components.

Psychologists may also hold a master's or Doctorate (Ph.D.) level qualification in psychology. In this case, they can call themselves doctors (Dr.), but they aren't medical doctors.

Currently, there is a controversy over the use of the word "patient" by non-medical doctors when they talk to or about the people they are providing talk therapy. Because dictionaries define the word "patient" as a person who is receiving medical treatment, and the only ones who can provide medical treatment are medical doctors, those who are not physicians shouldn't use the word "patient." This is a key point in the search for clarity. In the past, whenever I heard the word "patient," I immediately linked it to a physician.

To this end, several psychologists and therapists I've heard in the media use the word "client" instead. I've read that some other psychologists and therapists don't like the idea of using the word "client." In this case, I would say they're free to pick another word that would please their sensibilities. But leaving the word "patient" to the physicians will certainly help stop the confusion.

6.- What's the negative impact of the words depression, depressed, and antidepressant?

It is imperative that once and for all, we break the paradigms surrounding the words **depression, depressed, and**

antidepressant. We must address that such words are totally misleading.

The word **depression** is absolutely out of place when it comes to this life-threatening disease. This word doesn't convey the gravity of the ailment at all. The word depression sounds almost like an insult to the ones who have undergone the fury of this malady and the incapacitating suffering it inflicts on its victims.

It's a shame that in the 21st century, this killer plague is still identified with a name that sounds so insignificant compared to the real extent of the turmoil.

In his book *Darkness Visible* William Styron rates the word depression in a very descriptive way.

"... a noun with a bland tonality and lacking any magisterial presence, used indifferently to describe an economic decline or a rut in the ground, a true wimp of a word for such a major illness."

As a person who has survived clinical depression, I can say this pervasive disorder truly has little to do with sadness. It has nothing to do with low self-esteem, weakness of character, lack of willpower, loneliness, or self-destructive behavior, as is usually suggested. This ailment is as catastrophic as it is difficult to understand.

Whoever thinks it's an exaggeration to say that a severe case of MDD is capable of putting the strongest men and women ON THEIR KNEES has never had an experience of this kind. And for this reason, they lack the understanding that can only be obtained through personal, cognitive experience.

This malady is totally disabling and, indeed, beyond comprehension. Trying to have someone else understand it can be compared to trying to teach colors to a person who was born blind.

On the other hand, it's also inaccurate to call the patients **depressed** people. We are not sad people! Unhappiness is not a synonym for major depressive disorder. Rather, pathological sadness is a consequence of the disease but is not the central issue. Those who live with this organic disease know that the opposite of depression isn't happiness. It is energy. It is vitality that this apocalyptic malady drains from the core of our brains and, consequently, from our whole being, making it difficult for us even to exist. The correct way to identify people with this illness is to say, "People with depression, the illness," and not "depressed people."

Likewise, the word **antidepressant** sounds like anti-sadness medication. It is far from being that. Other nerve problems and neurological diseases are also treated with antidepressants. For example, chronic pain syndromes and neuropathic pain, migraine, and premenstrual syndrome, in addition to eating disorders, anxiety, and panic attacks, among others.

The above words are obstacles on the path to the fundamental understanding that major depression and generalized anxiety disorder are actual physical diseases. Choosing to handle these issues from a different angle has been preventing seriously ill people from figuring out what exactly was happening to them and from taking the appropriate treatment for their condition.

Consequently, many people are ending their lives without having a chance to know their tribulations had a cause and, as such, were coming from their biology. It's my duty to make it clear that patients of this kind shouldn't be expected to find themselves a solution to their suffering. What they need is a cure.

The time to amend these semantic flaws is overdue. We need to come up with new nomenclatures that will strongly convey the seriousness of this disease. Otherwise, more and more people, especially young, will continue dying as victims of bias stemming from a lack of accurate information.

"When it comes to basic meat and potatoes of human medical misery, there's nothing else like depression."

Dr. Robert Sapolsky

I reached out to social media, and in a chat room, I found a couple of comments about depression from actual sufferers of the illness. Here, they raised their voices to say how the misconceptions were directly affecting them:

Person A.- "Each time depression is used in place of sadness, I feel that the mental health community gets a little less credit like our diagnosis is equal to your everyday sadness. It makes me feel like I am not as strong as you. I can assure you that I am stronger than I have ever been. So please, next time you catch yourself thinking you are 'so depressed,' try to think of another way to describe how you really feel."

Person B.- "As someone who lives with depression, I take offense when a peer thinks they are 'depressed' because their boyfriend ignored them for a day or they received a bad grade on a test. Depression does not go away when we make up with our significant other or do extra credit to raise our grades. Depression lingers for weeks, months, or even years. Maybe what you are feeling is stress, sadness, or fatigue, but please do not use a serious medical diagnosis I fight every day as a synonym for sadness."

7.- Can signs of MDD show as early as in childhood?

In the U.S., depression is one of the most common disorders diagnosed in children. The statistics on children aged 3 – 17 years in 2016 is 4.4 percent (approximately 2.7 million).

Depression and anxiety have increased over time. The number of diagnoses among children aged 6 – 17 years increased from 5.4 percent in 2003 to 8 percent in 2007 and to 8.4 percent in 2011 – 2012.

After examining the events that had been unfolding before my eyes, I concluded that my anxiety and depression had been manifesting since I was a child. Before going over my childhood depression, I would like to present a couple of accounts I ran into on the internet. They caught my attention because of their similarities with the experiences I went through during my childhood years.

Person 1.- "As a child of nine years of age, I remember going through a time of several months of crying uncontrollably. I remember a small female classmate asking me why I was crying. I told her I didn't know. I couldn't control it. It was embarrassing, but nonetheless, I had no control over crying at this time in my life. It came from some deep, dark place inside me that was saying I did not belong as a person in the life I was having. I was given a small blue wax-tasting pill. After many pills, I finally swallowed what otherwise would not go down, and although I still had the problem, I stopped the crying."

Person 2.- "I had the same problem as a child, and I also could not explain what was going on. I'd be shaking uncontrollably, and it was extremely embarrassing, even more so when someone noticed. I wasn't particularly fragile, but that sad feeling wouldn't go away. At the time, when it was unbearable, my mother would give me diazepam (she took it herself for epilepsy with gardenal), and I'd calm down a little and get sleepy, but the issue itself remained until adulthood. It only got better when I was treated with antidepressants and benzodiazepines. I have depression from time to time and probably had episodes since I was a kid, but at the time, doctors only said that I was overly sensitive; it was part of my personality and wouldn't require any treatment. Well, suffice it to say during my childhood and teenage years, I went through hell a lot due to depression episodes. Only after my 30s did I find proper medical treatment combined with psychotherapy to alleviate the symptoms. Luckily, I now recognize the pre-symptoms and seek help before an episode. But I was often misdiagnosed and went through trial-and-error treatments and specialists before being correctly diagnosed."

*My Own Childhood Depression

I was about to start kindergarten. I was so excited and couldn't wait for that day. I loved the idea of going to school. Every time I saw my older siblings sitting at the table doing their homework, I would sit by their side and beg them to let me do schoolwork with them. At first, they dismissed me and continued with their tasks, but I insisted until they gave me a sheet of paper and a pencil and showed me how to draw circles and lines. When I finished, I always asked for more. I was always so proud of my work that when Mom arrived, I would run up to her, bursting with enthusiasm, and show her my schoolwork.

My first day of school arrived. I was very happy because I was finally going to school like my older siblings. Mom took me by the hand, and off we went. We got to the place. Two teachers were welcoming the children. They greeted us, shook my hand, and asked for my name. "My name is Evelyn," I replied with a big smile on my face. I was feeling excited. Mom exchanged a few words with the teachers, then she waved goodbye and left.

When I saw my mom walk away, everything changed. The excitement vanished in an instant. I became agitated. I felt a strong pressure on my chest. I panicked, and the heavy crying started. You might say most children experience separation anxiety on the first day of school, and it's true. But it was also true I wasn't like most children. You will understand as you continue reading.

I was terrified by the intense emotions I was experiencing. I never imagined I was going to feel this bad at school. I always thought

I would feel content. This same scenario repeated for on following days. As more children began to adapt to school, fewer and fewer cried. However, I felt the most anxious when I noticed no other child was crying but me.

As the days passed, I observed the other children. They looked happy. They laughed, talked to each other, and talked to the teacher; some walked around the classroom, some painted, others worked with clay, others scribbled on paper with crayons, etc. Sitting on my chair with my face down on the table, I cried, feeling bothered by the noise and the strong smell of crayons and playdough. All those children who at first cried together with me because they weren't feeling comfortable in that place were enjoying it now. I wondered why they could feel happy and I couldn't.

One day, I needed to go to the bathroom. I had to ask the teacher for permission, but I didn't dare. I thought and thought about how I would say it to her. Should I raise my hand to get her attention or stand up and go to her? What if she gets upset because I am interrupting her class? What if she says no? I kept wondering. I debated in my mind for a long time. When I couldn't hold it anymore, I stood up to go to her and ask for permission. But it was too late. When the teacher saw what had happened, she went to call another teacher. They both looked at me, looked at the floor, and talked to each other. I remained standing for quite a while, frozen with shame.

Every morning, I begged my mom not to take me to school. Sometimes, I even ran a fever. I guess my body knew it was the only way I could avoid school. I felt so relieved when it happened.

The day came when I totally refused to go to school. I threw myself on the floor and resisted being put in my school uniform. No one could lift me up from there. Everyone was trying to convince me to go to school. My siblings promised me candy, a new toy, and to take me to places upon my return from school, etc. But there was no way to convince me. I just couldn't stand the way I felt when I was at school. However, Mom knew it wasn't possible for me to stay home because she had to go to work, and all my older siblings were going to school, too. There was nobody left to watch me. Then, Mom used one last resource to persuade me; she told me I would have to stay at school for only half a day. She said she would pick me up at lunchtime. I asked her to promise me. Looking into my eyes, she made the promise. I agreed to go to school that day.

Mom's promise stayed with me all morning. The simple thought of having to stay at school for half a day only, instead of eight hours or so, calmed down my anxiety considerably. Midday arrived. There was a small group of children who were picked up at noon by lunchtime. It seems their parents didn't trust the quality of the food served at school. Because in Perú, the main meal is lunch, these parents preferred their children to have it at home.

The children who were leaving for lunch were to wait for their parents near the front door. I approached the teacher in charge and told her my mom was going to pick me up to go have lunch at home. She asked for my name. She looked at her list and said, "You are not on the list, sweetie." I insisted. "My mom promised she would pick me up at this time." Then the teacher said, "OK, wait over here." The minutes passed, and my mother did not arrive. Soon, all the other children were gone, and I was still waiting. Finally, the teacher told me I should go back to my classroom because it didn't seem my mom was coming. "But my mom promised me," I insisted. "I know she is coming because she promised me." But my mom never showed up. That afternoon, I cried more than ever.

Neither my mom nor my teachers could understand how serious my struggle was, maybe because, as adults, we think little children don't have serious problems. At such an early age, I had been left alone to fight this huge monster. This anxiety was way stronger than me.

(Mom lied to me for two reasons. First, because she didn't have a choice, she needed to go to work, and there was nobody at home to watch me. And second, because she might have thought I would forget about it as the morning passed by.

Back home, I didn't complain to Mom for breaking her promise. Maybe I was afraid she would get mad at me. She never brought up the topic, either. I realized she had totally forgotten about it. To her eyes, it was definitely not a big deal.

Now, as an adult, I understand that Mom couldn't know better because nobody had taught her. She lost her own mother when she was only thirteen years old).

For several weeks, I continued struggling to adjust to school. I finally understood that the situation wasn't going to change. I would have to continue attending kindergarten, and there was nothing I could do about it. I made the effort to start participating in class. I remember working on playdough while I was still crying. And I would see the sheets of paper I was coloring get wet with my tears.

This painful process of adjustment took time, but it finally ended. I started learning, and eventually, I enjoyed school a lot.

At the end of the school year, I was awarded a diploma in recognition of having obtained the highest score in achievement and behavior in my class. Because of that, the teacher allowed me to be the first to walk to the table where all the end-of-year presents had been placed so I could choose my gift. I was thrilled!

At dismissal, my older sister Mayra came to pick me up. She had come along with a friend of hers, both still wearing their school uniforms. When my sister saw me coming out holding my diploma, she got so excited. She hugged me tightly, and we both jumped with joy. Then, she turned to her friend and said, "See? I told you my sister was going to be awarded the diploma!"

And so, like the happy girl I should've always been, I started running home. I couldn't wait to get there to show Mom my diploma and make her feel proud of me.

CHAPTER 2

AT THE PSYCHIATRIC WARD

WHAT ARE DAYS LIKE AT A PSYCH WARD?

The days started between 7:00 and 7:30. Breakfast was served around 8:00, so we had to show up in the dining room by that time if we wanted to eat. They never forced anybody to eat, but the nurses recommended doing it so we wouldn't take the medication on an empty stomach. Everybody was given some medication, pills, or tablets. At the time, I didn't know exactly what kind of medicine it was. All I knew was that it calmed my nerves. These pills quickly relaxed my muscle tension. At present, I know they weren't antidepressants because that kind of medication doesn't have a calming effect.

The premises had sitting areas with shelves containing books, magazines, and board games. Reading books also helped me release tension, at least temporarily, and playing board games was a way of socializing.

Patients were scheduled for daily activities at the hospital. After breakfast and taking our medication, we would do something. One day, we were to do some artwork. They provided us with paper, pencils, colored pencils, and crayons. It was like being in preschool when the teachers gave us paints and brushes to keep us entertained.

We sat at long dining tables. There were about a dozen people in the room, so it was tumultuous. The truth is that having to do something like that made me feel silly. I couldn't see any value in doing kids' stuff. Nonetheless, I decided to just go with the flow. So, I took a pencil and an eraser and started drawing.

Esteban and Pablo, two hospital inmates, didn't seem to like the idea either. They just scribbled on the paper and talked, pretending they were participating. I, however, kept working and ended up drawing a puppy dog. It was a small hairy thing with eyes half-covered by its light-brown fur. It was standing on two legs and sticking its tongue out, like when they wanted attention from their masters. I made the puppy's tongue pink and added some black spots. Upon finishing my masterpiece, I handed it to the counselors, who, by the way, loved it, and so they posted it on the bulletin board.

Individual talk sessions with a psychologist were among the services provided. The first talk therapy I had was about learning to modify or change negative thoughts to improve my emotional experiences. It also discussed the importance of having a positive attitude toward life and the need to focus on solutions rather than problems.

Soon, I had already started a kind of friendship with my fellow hospital inmates, Esteban, Pablo, Julia, and Elena. I liked conversing with Esteban and Pablo because they were both very friendly and entertaining. They usually had something funny to say, and I needed to distract my mind and get away from myself.

One afternoon after finishing lunch, as we were leaving the dining room, Julia came along. She looked very upset.

"Someone stole my pack of cigarettes," she said.

Julia smoked multiple times during the day, so her cigarettes were precious to her.

"I think I know who the thief is," she affirmed. She pointed and said, "See that woman, the one with an eye patch? She is the thief; she stole my cigarettes."

"Calm down, Julia," said Esteban. "What makes you think it was her? Did you see her do it?"

"No. But I know she's the thief. Can't you see she's smoking right now?"

"Don't accuse without evidence," added Elena. Maybe you dropped the pack somewhere, or it may be among your belongings. Look again."

"I've already looked, and it's nowhere to be found. But this bitch is going to get to know me, " Julia threatened. Without another word, she went to confront the woman.

"Thief! You stole my cigarettes. You thought I wasn't going to catch you, right? Give me back my pack of cigarettes."

The lady looked very puzzled. And without saying a single word, she fled the place very scared.

"Did you see? It was her; that's why she ran because she's guilty," said Julia.

Finally, we managed to calm her down, and we all forgot about the incident.

By the end of the day, Julia confessed that she had found her pack of cigarettes among her belongings. But first, she made me promise not to tell anyone so she wouldn't have to apologize.

Narrative Therapy was another activity scheduled at the clinic. We participated in group sessions in which we could talk about our personal struggles. The therapist suggested that sharing our stories and difficulties could help us release anxiety, and it could also be a way to give each other emotional support. He asked us to volunteer only if we felt comfortable talking before the group.

Julia raised her hand to volunteer. She started her story by saying she was an alcoholic and also addicted to cigarettes. She talked about how she had stayed in an abusive relationship because of her love for her husband, only to find out that in addition to mistreating her, he was also cheating on her. She turned to cigarettes and alcohol because they helped her feel her problems weren't as serious.

While listening to her story, I imagined how bad she must have felt all that time, and I felt sorry for her. Although I didn't justify her behavior, I was able to understand her. Even though her problems had nothing to do with mine, we both had something in common. We were both struggling. I started feeling close to her, as if I had known her for a while.

The next volunteer was Esteban. He wasn't quite thirty, tall, handsome, and, as mentioned above, he had a good sense of humor. Before he started talking, I wondered what could be happening to this strong and muscular guy that had brought him to a place like this.

He soon began telling his story. "People who know me say I have a nice personality and a good sense of humor. Maybe I am funny, and I am an extrovert, but what I can't say is that I am a free man. I have ties." The tone of his voice changed, and his facial expression became serious. Then he continued, "At this stage in my life, I'm fighting a very tough battle against my drug addiction. That's why, like all of you, I'm here looking for healing. I need some guidance that will lead me to find my way back to what my life was before the drugs...."

As Esteban was telling his story, I was stunned by the fact that this young man, who emanated charm on the outside and who looked happy, could also be going through serious internal life struggles. Although we had opposite personalities, we also had something in common: we both were confronting our difficulties and seemed to be willing to do whatever it took to conquer them.

Early the morning after, I was looking out the window of my room when I saw Esteban and Pablo standing outside the building, ringing the doorbell. They were wearing sneakers, sweatshirts, and pants. They looked fatigued and sweaty. They must have gone for a run, I thought. Then, I tucked my head out the window and yelled, "Hey, I didn't know we were allowed to leave the premises."

"We're not," Esteban answered.

"So, why did they let you guys out?"

"Because we are men!" Pablo replied. Then, both of them laughed out loud.

In another session with the psychologist, she presented a series of cards containing abstract drawings. Upon showing each flashcard, she asked, "What might this be?"

I had no idea why the psychologist wanted me to identify the drawings. Nonetheless, I observed each one of the cards and expressed what they looked like to me. I remember seeing things like a butterfly, tiny animals, flowers...

Little did I know at the time this was a projective personality test, the RORSCHACH Test. This test employs ten bilaterally symmetrical inkblot cards. According to its inventor, a Swiss psychiatrist and psychoanalyst named Dr. Hermann Rorschach, when we provide our perception or perspective on ambiguous images, we are genuinely revealing elements of our personality. We are supposedly showing how we project meaning onto the real world (as long as we don't know what it is about in advance, of course).

This test must have some value because it revealed that I am sensitive, caring, and family-oriented. And I know it is true.

ARE ALL PATIENTS IN PSYCH CLINICS MENTALLY ILL?

It was Valentine's Day in Lima-Perú, and the nurses had organized a small party. In addition to celebrating love and friendship, I guessed that they intended to keep the patients engaged and entertained.

It was almost time for the party. Elena and I were talking. In a dismissive tone of voice, she said, "Evelyn, are you going to the party?"

"I don't think so," I answered in a disinterested voice. "I have nothing to celebrate," I said and shrugged my shoulders with annoyance.

"I also prefer to stay and read a book," answered Elena.

"If I go to the party, it'll be just to pretend I'm having fun," I added.

At that moment, Pablo and Julia came along. They seemed to be in a good mood. Pablo, in a funny tone and with a big smile, tried to persuade us to attend the event.

"Ladies, we are waiting for you; we are here to escort you."

"Now, boring girls, move on," Julia added, haranguing us.

"I'm not attracted to this type of celebration," Elena replied.

"Neither am I," said Julia, smiling. "But there will be food, and I'm starving."

Pablo insisted, "I understand being in a place like this makes us feel down. But it is precisely why we should look for some distraction. Besides, we must be grateful to all the people who have given themselves the task of organizing an event for us. We can't let them down."

Given so much insistence, we decided to attend.

The room was decorated with streamers. There were balloons on the walls, too. I saw sandwiches and soft drinks on the table. They were also playing trendy salsa music which I have always loved.

I pulled up a chair and sat down. Pablo came over and offered me a cigarette. No thanks, I replied. "Me neither," said Elena. "I would take a beer if I could."

"Give me two," said Julia. "I love smoking. It calms my nerves. I can't live without my cigarettes."

"I'll take one," said Esteban. "Cigarettes help me relax, too, although I have been cutting back on them."

From my seat, I dedicated myself to observing the behavior of the other hospital inmates attending the party.

"Hey, look at Lola! What has she put on her head? It looks like a turban," exclaimed Julia, laughing.

Lola danced by herself, round and round, and yet what looked like a turban never fell off her head.

There was the lady with a patch over one of her eyes. We had no idea what had happened to her.

Esteban whispered, commenting on her, "Hey, she sure thought it was a costume party, so she dressed as a pirate." We all laughed out loud.

I shook my head as a sign that I disapproved of his comment. However, I couldn't help but laugh, too.

Then I could see a man, short and kind of old. He danced and smoked a cigarette at the same time, in addition to making smoke rings in the air.

I could also see another woman dancing expeditiously and not following the rhythm of the music they were playing- definitely in her very own style. Anyway, the important thing is that she was having fun. Shortly thereafter, she lost her balance, tripped, and ended up on the floor.

Our first reaction was to laugh, but immediately after, we went to help her up. Fortunately, it was nothing serious.

In the end, we didn't have as bad a time as we had thought. Indeed, we had some fun.

It was time for the subsequent group therapy, and I found myself interested in listening to what the other patients had to say. Throughout the few sessions I attended, I heard several life stories, some more tragic than others. I thought the people who shared their struggles were so brave. It takes a lot of courage to stand in front of other people you hardly know and expose your inner, most private conflicts.

The therapist asked for a volunteer who would like to share their story. I didn't take the chance to talk because I felt I could benefit more from listening to other people's experiences than from talking about mine. I realized that when I focused on other people's struggles, I could divert my attention away from my own.

On this occasion, Pablo volunteered. He began by saying, "My wife and I always wanted to have two children. I dreamed for the first to be a boy, which would make me very happy. We had our first child, but it wasn't a boy. I felt kind of disappointed. Nonetheless, as our daughter grew older, she got more and more beautiful, and I grew to love her deeply. When I came home from work, she ran to the door with open arms, yelling, "Daddy, daddy!" and waiting for me to pick her up. I adored her.

A few years later, we had another child—this time, a boy! We felt extremely fortunate.

Time passed, and our beautiful daughter was about to turn fifteen. She dreamed of a big party and a princess dress for that day. Therefore, I promised her the most beautiful party she could imagine. My wife found her dream dress for that occasion.

One day, we received a call from her school. They informed us that our daughter was feeling sick, and we had to go pick her up. We took her to the hospital, and they ran some tests. The doctor told us she had a kidney infection, and although it was not serious, she should start treatment with medicine.

Days passed by, but she was not improving. Again, the doctor reassured us that it was nothing we should worry about much. He said sometimes it took longer for some patients to respond to treatment.

More tests followed, and her health wasn't improving. At this point, it was apparent her long-awaited party wasn't going to take place when it should. My beautiful girl was heartbroken. My wife and I felt so frustrated for not being able to fulfill our daughter's desire to have her dream sweet-fifteen party.

She was kept in treatment for a few more weeks. I finally confronted the doctor over the fact that I was not seeing my girl improving. He told us she was currently not responding to treatment, and because of that, he was changing medications.

Things turned for the worse. I got so desperate that I went to see the doctor and complained to him, telling him he hadn't taken my daughter's case seriously, he had misled us when he kept saying it was not serious, and he hadn't acted promptly when he saw the medicines were not helping her. I was furious at the doctor. I yelled and screamed at him out of desperation.

I went to church and got down on my knees, begging for my daughter's life and the opportunity to fulfill her dream of wearing that beautiful dress that was waiting for her. I cried and cried, begging God not to take my daughter away from me… My prayers weren't heard. She passed away a little after turning fifteen."

At that moment, most of us present were covering our mouths with our hands with wide open, watery eyes. In silence, we looked at each other in disbelief.

After Pablo's account, I learned that physical appearance says very little about who we really are. Previously, I only saw in Pablo a muscular man, imposing, like a rock that could hardly break. But now I could see that even strong men can break in the face of a tragedy of this nature. I also understood that somewhere else in the world, there is always someone going through greater pain than ours.

It was time to sleep. I was lying in bed thinking about all I had heard about other people's misery. Then, I reflected on my own life. "What is my story?" I wondered. "What is the reason for my struggles?" Nothing was clear to me. Reflecting on my own reality, I closed my eyes and started bringing back memories:

… It's six in the morning, and the alarm clock goes off. I jump out of bed and go take a shower. I am trying to get dressed as soon as possible so I can get to work on time. However, time was almost always short for me to fix myself so that I could look as good as I wanted.

"Have your breakfast, Evelyn," says my mom. "Try to hurry up getting dressed, or you won't have time to eat."

"Mom, I work in an office; I must dress nicely," I said. "I still need to touch up my nails!"

Then I turned to my sisters. "Hey, I'm missing a ring from my jewelry box. Has anyone seen it?

And there is only one of the earrings I want to wear today, what a bummer!

Who is taking my things? I can't go without my earrings and my rings..."

Right after turning nineteen, I started working as an office assistant and receptionist. In the evening, I went to school. I was studying to become a teacher of English. I felt happy, eager to get ahead and leave behind all those years of shortages in which I grew up. I was convinced I had already placed myself on the correct path where my life should lead. The future was very promising; all I needed was to study and work hard, which didn't scare me in the least.

The environment at work was entertaining, vibrant, and engaging. In a short period of time, I developed a great friendship with three of my coworkers, Clarissa, Lilian, and Maria. We became inseparable, and together we went to every social event that any one of us had been invited to. Some weekends we went to a disco or out for pizza. Other times we shopped almost all day, and then we went for food, etc. We were energized.

In the office, Mila was my direct boss. At first, she seemed too serious and strict to me. But she was also very dedicated to her work, and she had years of experience. I was just starting out in the workplace. Nonetheless, soon, Mila went from being my direct boss to being a close friend.

A year or so passed after I started working in the office. Soon after, I got back pain. It kept happening until it was really bothering me. I mentioned it to Mila.

"You know what, Mila, my back has been hurting for several days. It feels tight; it hurts when I make sudden moves. What could it be?"

"Maybe you don't sit in the right position," Mila replied. "When you spend a lot of time sitting at a desk, your back can get tired, and your muscles ache."

"It might be. I'll try to remember always to sit up straight so this pain will go away," I replied.

The backache kept coming and going, and it was annoying when it happened. Months later, new symptoms started showing up. I was feeling tired on a daily basis. I thought it was normal. I was working all day and going to school in the evening. Of course, I was tired. I wasn't sleeping well, either. I'd wake up in the middle of the night, and then it was difficult to fall back asleep. I also got a cold-like allergy frequently. After months of feeling uneasy, I finally decided to visit the doctor. At the doctor's office, I described my physical symptoms. The doctor asked several questions regarding my health and my lifestyle.

After running the checkup, he commented, "At first glance, I don't see anything out of the ordinary. But although your weight is still in the normal range, you are very skinny. Have you been losing weight without trying?"

"No. I've always been skinny, the skinniest among all my siblings. By the way, I have nine."

The doctor continued, "Maybe you aren't eating well. Have you lost your appetite?"

"Not at all. I love food, and I eat a good amount, but for some reason, I don't put on weight."

"Anyway," said the doctor, "I'm going to order some blood tests. We need to rule out anemia. Meanwhile, you could start taking a B12 vitamin. It can help you sleep better and regain energy."

"And what should I do about my allergy?"

"You should take vitamin C. It can help you with it."

"All right," I agreed. "I will start taking vitamin B12 and vitamin C as you have suggested."

"Fine. So, let's have the test done, and I'll see again when I get the results."

I left the office quite positive. A few days later, the tests came out negative. I felt relieved to know I was not sick. I went on with my life, enjoying everything I was doing.

After a few more months of following my routine between work and school, my sense of well-being began to fade again, and new problems arose.

One night, I woke up with a terrible stomachache. I got up to make some herbal tea for indigestion, but the pain didn't subside. Rather, it became more and more intense. So, I took some OTC medicine as well. But nothing made me feel better.

The pain became so intense that they had to take me to the emergency room.

At the ER, they ran some lab tests. After waiting long hours, the doctor let us know all the tests came out normal. In conclusion, it was only indigestion. They gave me a shot of pain medicine and recommended rest with some food restrictions.

It was dawn already when Mom and I returned home. I couldn't go to work or attend my classes for the day. When I did go back to work, my inseparable friends asked me about my health. It made me feel good to see they cared, and I thanked them deeply.

My dear friends worried in their own way, of course. Clarissa approached first. "Darling, what happened? Did you get sick? You probably ate very late at night."

"That wasn't the case this time. I ate at the usual time."

Lila started with her jokes. "I think you made yourself sick to miss work. Come on, confess!"

Maria played along. "What a good idea! I think next week I'm going to do the same. I must get sick on a Friday so I can have a long weekend sunbathing on the beach!"

I couldn't help but laugh. "You and your jokes! Are you guys ever going to take something seriously?"

My health issues had come to stay. I started getting strep throat regularly. And every time, I was prescribed antibiotics. I knew taking antibiotics too frequently wasn't ideal, but there was no other way for me to get rid of the infection.

A month or so had passed since I had the first episode of intense stomachache. For a second time, I woke up with a serious stomachache that got more and more intense. This time, I was also throwing up. I put up with the pain for a couple of hours, hoping it would go away on its own. But it didn't happen, so I was rushed to the ER again.

Like on the previous occasion, they ran some tests, but nothing strange was found in my system. The doctor instructed me to eliminate various foods from my diet. They gave me another injection for the pain and a consultation to see a gastroentero-logist.

I was very worried about having to miss another day of work. I felt I was putting my job at risk. Work was scarce, so having a formal job was like winning the lottery in my city! And I needed to work so I could pay for school. But after not having slept all night, I just couldn't go to work. One thing was very clear: I wasn't going to go see the specialist any time soon. I wouldn't miss work once more.

I spent several weeks on diets and food restrictions. When I saw everyone else in my house eating all that delicious food mom made, which I couldn't eat, I felt nostalgic, frustrated, and isolated. But I'd also think of those horrible stomachaches that had brought me down. And I always had in mind I could no longer miss work or school. With a lot of willpower, I managed to resist the temptation to eat all the food I loved, and for quite some time, I adhered to the diet recommended by the doctor.

A few months passed. It was a Sunday, and I had invited Dante, my boyfriend, to have lunch with us. My mom cooked a delicious Peruvian dish everyone in my house loved, chicken and cilantro stew.

"Delicious," Dante exclaimed, "This chicken and cilantro stew is just perfect, outstanding!"

"Mom, you always make a delicious chicken and cilantro stew, but today it's superb," I added.

"Thank you. I'm glad you like it. Would you like some more, Dante?"

"Sure. Thank you."

We all enjoyed the finger-licking lunch Mom had cooked.

Later, we sat down and watched a comedy series, *El Chavo del Ocho (The Boy of House # 8)*, on TV. It was everybody's favorite because it was very funny. We all laughed our heads off every time we watched it, and this time was no exception.

I was enjoying the day until my stomach started hurting. I got alarmed. Thinking I might go through the same hassle made me nervous. Again, I had herbal teas and then as many OTC medicines as possible to relieve indigestion. I was terrified at the possibility of having to miss work once more.

The following day, I was still feeling bad. Despite that, I left for my office. Practically, my whole life depended on my job, so I was determined to attend, even if I had to drag myself to get there. This health problem was robbing me of my inner peace and settling more and more stress on me. It was high time I saw the gastroenterologist.

After telling the specialist all the trouble I had been going through, he ordered a colonoscopy. I was twenty-one, and I got an order for a test that, at the time, was carried out at age fifty. Because of that, my insurance wouldn't cover such a test. I had to pay out of pocket, which significantly impacted my finances.

Before the colonoscopy, there were more food restrictions. The preparation for the test happened to be very problematic. Three days prior, I needed to eat rice mainly. On the day before, I had to drink this prescription liquid aimed to cleanse my intestines. I had to drink it multiple times during the day. This liquid caused me stomach cramps and made me nauseous. It was a stressful process that made me feel sick for the most part of the day.

I finally had the colonoscopy, and I felt some relief at this point. Nonetheless, after having spent almost all day between going to the hospital, having the test itself done, and waiting for the results, the doctor informed me they had found nothing abnormal. Everything was fine!

I felt mortified. So much time taken off, so much money and effort for nothing!

It was the beginning of a new year, and I was still restricting certain foods. I was so scared of indigestion that I got to the point where I would only eat toast and tea all day. In the mornings, I woke up tired with the sensation of not having slept at all. As time passed by, new symptoms were added to the existing ones. My feet grew heavy, and my legs hurt.

Since the problems with my digestive system wouldn't go away, the doctor ordered more tests. This time for the gallbladder.

I had to take one more day off work to go have the test done. They took X-rays of my stomach, then they gave me a chocolate bar to eat. Minutes later, they retook X-rays. The goal was to measure the changes in my gallbladder after ingesting the chocolate.

The gastroenterologist read the report in my presence. "The first image taken of the gallbladder reveals normal size and anatomy. The second image taken after ingesting the chocolate reveals the reaction within regular parameters. In conclusion, nothing abnormal was found."

The news was supposed to relieve me, but I was rather annoyed. I felt tired. I had taken so many steps just to end up at the same point from where I started.

I looked the doctor in the eyes and asked, "Is there any other test that can be done? I think we should keep looking until we find the problem."

"I don't think so. The tests they have run are enough; all the results indicate there's nothing abnormal."

It sounded weird to me to hear I was healthy while I was feeling ill most of the time.

"Maybe you are stressed out," he concluded. "Try not to think about your health problems, and they may go away."

I felt lost. What was left to do now?

My dear friends knew about all my visits to the doctors and the several health tests they had run on me, so when I went to the office the following day, this time too, they wanted to know about the latest results.

"So again, they told you there's nothing wrong with you? Who can feel ill because of NOTHING?!" Lila exclaimed.

Maria said, "This is not only weird but also annoying. You have spent a lot of money on specialty doctors and tests, in addition to the income you have lost from missing work all those days. So much money for nothing!"

"Do not despair, Evelyn," said Clarissa in a calm tone. "There is always something else we can do. I have an idea that can help us clear the mystery."

"Really?" I said. "What do you suggest?"

"Easy," Clarissa continued, "ask your doctor to perform an AUTOPSY!"

"What?!" we all exclaimed.

With a big smile on her face, Clarissa said, "Yes, an autopsy. You aren't going to survive, but at least we'll know what you died of."

We all laughed uproariously. We couldn't stop laughing. My crazy, funny buddies always managed to make me laugh, even when I was feeling upset. I loved them dearly.

It was time for another annual checkup. This doctor was seeing me for the first time. I told him everything that had been happening with my health. After reviewing my records, the doctor made some comments.

"I see your digestive problem is recurring. They have already done several tests, and everything seems to be fine. Is this right?"

"According to the exams, nothing is wrong with me. However, I'm not feeling well. I have less energy; I go to bed tired and wake up just as tired. Getting out of bed in the morning demands much effort."

"I see you don't have anemia either. I'm going to give you an order for routine tests and see if something has changed. Perhaps your job is very demanding, and it's robbing you of your energy. What do you do?"

"I'm an office assistant. Doctor, I don't think my job is demanding. I'm very pleased with what I do."

"What do you do after work?"

"I go to school."

"Your days are long. Maybe you should take a break, either from work or school, and give yourself some time to rest and relax."

"But my problem isn't work or school; the problem is my health issues. What I want is to feel healthy, with energy to be able to do even more things."

"Do you exercise?"

"I like going for walks, but I don't work out."

"Maybe walking isn't enough. Start doing exercise. It can help boost your energy levels."

"All right. That I can do."

"As for your stomach pain, it may be stress. Are you the kind of person who worries too much about everything?"

"I do worry about my future, but I don't think I worry too much."

"I am prescribing B-12 vitamin. I think it can help you."

"I took B12 for some time in the past, but I didn't feel any different."

"You will need to take it for a longer period of time."

The doctor continued, "I'm going to wait for the test results. If we find something wrong, we'll be calling you."

I had been hoping the doctor would suggest other possible reasons for my uneasy feelings. Why would it be due to stress if I was having a good time at work?

I started working out, as the doctor suggested. But all I got from exercising was feeling more tired. My discomfort wouldn't go away. I thought about going to see another doctor, but I realized there was no point. It was almost certain they weren't going to find anything wrong, and once again, I would be reassured that I was in perfect health.

As time passed, my interest in spending time with Dante, my boyfriend, faded away, too. So was my desire for intimacy. Sometimes, I felt sex was silly and, at a certain point, even annoying. I found myself making excuses so I wouldn't have to go out with Dante. Sometime after, I broke up with him.

I started doubting myself. I began to think maybe everything was just in my head; maybe the belief that there was something wrong was causing my anxiety and stress. To tell the truth, I was feeling stressed, but it had all started with my health issues, not the way around. Anyway, I thought maybe it was a matter of keeping myself busy and distracted most of the time so I wouldn't think about my health problems.

On weekdays, I tried to fill all my hours with extra activities like working overtime or studying an extra hour. On the weekends, I spent long hours cleaning my house and tidying up my bedroom in detail. Other times, I took everything out of the refrigerator, cleaned it thoroughly, and then reorganized every single item.

Week after week, I kept pushing myself. But nothing got easier. As a matter of fact, everything was getting even worse as the months passed by. The bacterial infection in my throat was also recurring. The otolaryngologist suggested it was caused by my allergies. I had a weird allergy to anything cold. I couldn't eat ice cream, drink cold soda, or even cold water. "Allergies are like a curse," the doctor commented. "You can never get rid of them."

Next, the daytime drowsiness started. I had to constantly try to keep my eyes open. Trying to give the impression that I was feeling well was terribly exhausting! I had been told so many times there was nothing wrong with me that I felt I shouldn't allow myself to think otherwise. I needed to believe the despair would subside if I gave it some time. But in reality, I was going downward steadily.

As almost everything has a limit, I was about to reach mine. I had turned into a ticking bomb, almost ready to explode. And the moment came. This was the time I was admitted to the psych clinic.

*Motion sickness and MDD

Around this same time, when other symptoms of major depression had started to manifest, motion sickness added to them.

One morning, while riding the bus to work, I opened my book and began to review my lessons, just as I did every day. While reading my notebook, I started to feel like my head was bulging. Something very strange, difficult to explain. I stopped reading, lifted my face, closed my eyes, and took deep breaths to relax. Then, I continued my reading. A few minutes passed, and I started to feel a little dizzy. I tried to ignore the discomfort, but it started to intensify. I got to feeling so dizzy that even while sitting, it seemed like I was going to fall. I started to feel nauseous and was about to throw up. I felt I couldn't allow this to happen since I was on a bus full of people, and I didn't even have a plastic bag within my reach. I thought about getting up and getting off the bus, but I had no stability. It was very possible that I would fall if I tried. I felt trapped. My anxiety started rising rapidly, like foam in a soda drink when it's poured into a glass. I slipped into a state of panic. As a survival measure, all I could do was tilt my head back and begin to inhale air through my nose and exhale through my mouth as slowly as possible. I stayed in this position throughout the remainder of my trip. Those were the longest minutes of my life so far.

Finally, I got to my stop, got off the bus, and ran behind the bench wall where there was dirt, and I vomited. I felt relieved after that, but I also felt so embarrassed. I kept feeling uneasy for the rest of the day.

After this incident, I've never again been able to read while in a moving vehicle. Every time I accidentally read something while my husband is driving, I feel sick to my stomach. More than once, the rest of my day was ruined. It can get that serious.

The National Institute of Health defines motion sickness as follows, "Motion sickness is a common and complex syndrome that occurs in response to either real or perceived motion. Its presentation can be diverse and may include the gastrointestinal, central nervous system, and autonomic symptoms… The exact neurobiological cause of motion sickness is unclear.…"

At the back of our heads, we have a fist-sized part of the brain called the **cerebellum.** The main functions of the cerebellum are to maintain posture, balance, and equilibrium. It also coordinates voluntary muscle movements. There is scientific evidence that people with MDD have a smaller cerebellum. This could be another possible reason for my loss of balance, dizziness, and lack of stability.

~ ~ ~

After reviewing my life prior to my arrival at the psychiatric ward, I went back to the time at the hospital.

It was early evening. We had just finished having dinner when one of the nurses approached me and said she needed to talk to me. We sat down, and then she told me a new patient had been admitted, and she was going to be my roommate.

"All right," I said, a little concerned. "But let me ask you, are you sure this lady isn't going to get mad like the one who scared me the other morning?"

"Oh, no," the nurse said. "Don't be concerned. She has a different problem. This patient is seriously ill with depression. I believe you, as a patient with depression too, can understand this lady better."

"Sure," I replied. "I hope I can offer her some help."

When I got into the room, she was lying in bed. She had been given a shot of anxiolytics to have her sleep. When the effect wore off, she woke up.

"Hi, my name is Evelyn. I'm your roommate. What's your name?"

"Adelina," she replied.

"If you need anything, just let me know, and I'll go find the nurse."

"Thank you," she said. Her voice trembled.

I noticed her lips were dry, so I offered her some water. Then, I helped her sit up and drink it.

She thanked me again. She sounded weak. Right after, her eyes filled with tears, and she couldn't stop them from rolling down her cheeks.

I took her hands and caressed them gently over and over to make her feel she was not alone. I told her it was okay for her to cry and that crying might help ease her pain.

Then, her crying turned into deep sobbing. I felt like I should hug her, so I did. I rubbed her back for a few moments. Then, as most of us would react in a situation like this, I felt the need to say something. But what? I didn't know what would be appropriate. I was afraid I would say something wrong that might make her feel even worse. Some things I had heard before came to my mind. I wasn't convinced those words were true, but I thought maybe they would help her.

"Mrs. Adelina, I don't know what ails you, but I assure you it's temporary; it will pass. Time heals everything. Do you have children?"

"I have two boys. A nine-year-old and an eleven-year-old."

"Who are your children with at this moment?"

"With my husband. He is a very good father and husband. He has brought me here because although all my family has been trying to help me, I'm getting worse. I just can't handle what is happening. It's too much for me."

"I have heard for every problem; there's a solution. There must be one for yours."

Without realizing it, I had gone from being just another patient to being a counselor.

"There's no solution for mine." She answered.

"Listen, I see you have three great reasons to live. Not many women are blessed with a loving husband and two little angels."

"I know. I feel guilty because my kids need me, and I'm not there for them. I'm not strong enough to get out of this hole. I'm a failure…."

Adelina was getting more anxious. My goodness! I felt I shouldn't have opened my mouth. I held her hands tight and tried to say something different.

"Calm down, Adelina. I'm sure you are the best mother. You just need more time. Your kids are well taken care of; you shouldn't worry about them for now. You need some rest, and soon you'll be able to leave the bad times in the past."

"Today, I feel the past is going to haunt me forever. I wish I could change the past. I wish I could've prevented certain things from happening."

"Something terrible must've happened to make you feel so engulfed in such pain."

She continued. "I grew up in a little town in one of the country's provinces. Despite our poverty, my siblings and I grew up under the protection of our parents. Unfortunately, both my parents died fairly young. I was the oldest of three, but I was very young too. They left behind my baby sister. I became her mother, I raised her like my own daughter, and I have always loved her that way.

At age seventeen, my baby sister fell in love with a man ten years her senior. She never told me about it. I found out about the relationship when it was too late. She was pregnant already. Later, we learned this man was married and had other children. We went to look for him, but we couldn't find him anywhere. He had gone into hiding. My sister was looking for him, too. Unfortunately, she managed to find him before us. She asked for an explanation about why he had lied to her.

I can't imagine what horrible things that bastard must've told her that left her so devastated. She wouldn't tell.

Sometime after, my sister killed herself... She ingested rat poison."

At that moment, I felt an intense cold run through my veins, and I thought, "OMG! Poor woman, what a catastrophe!"

I was speechless. I felt there was nothing I could say to ease her anguish at this point. After all, I was just a young woman in my early twenties trying to reassure someone much older.

After what I had just heard, I felt ashamed of myself. Ashamed of believing my pain was too hard. I could even consider myself lucky amid so much misfortune.

The following day, Adelina's husband and her two sons came to visit. I got to meet them. The husband looked really concerned, and her two kids were visibly sad.

We shared the room for two nights. Thereafter, they moved me to another section of the hospital, into a room with three beds instead of two; I never asked why. I didn't get to see Adelina again.

SLEEPING PILLS FOR HORSES?

At night, we all had to be in bed at eight. Shortly after taking the sleeping medicine, all lights would go out. We weren't supposed to talk or make noise after that. Since I could sleep for around four or five hours only, I had the rest of the night just for thinking. I wished I could've at least been able to read books.

The nights were cold, long, and tedious for me. I spent hour after hour staring at the ceiling and hearing the deep breathing of the other two roommates, who slept through the night without any trouble. If only I could have slept like that!

The doors to the rooms remained open all night. I think they wanted to monitor the patients and make sure no one was doing anything wrong, like hurting ourselves, I guess.

From my room, I could see the nurse on duty sitting behind a desk. A dim light illuminated the space where she was located. She was leaning over the counter, looking down. Apparently, she was reading or writing something, and from time to time, she walked past the rooms to check us out.

On the following night, I did something I couldn't suspect would leave another disturbing impression on my already struggling emotional life. I decided to speak with the doctor on duty. I explained to him how difficult it was for me to fall asleep and stay asleep. I asked if he could increase the dose of the sleeping pills I was taking. Without hesitating, the doctor agreed to do so. I was so grateful!

After taking the new dose, I miraculously fell asleep within minutes. When I woke up, it was already daylight. I had slept through the night. I just couldn't believe it! This was big for me; I had finally found a way to end my long, tedious nights, which had been causing me so much frustration. What a relief!

Upon awakening, I turned to my roommates and told them I was so grateful for not having gone through another horrible night without being able to sleep. Then, I got out of bed and stood up. With a big smile on my face, I looked up, stretching my arms vigorously from side to side.

Unfortunately, my contentment was cut short abruptly by a thunderous noise that made the ground shake. Afterward, I heard someone yelling for the nurse. The place got noisy; I could hear people talking, but I couldn't really understand what they were saying. I felt the floor shake a little bit again. It was caused by some people running. A nurse rushed into my room. She kneeled by my side. Then, she held my left arm and proceeded to lift my head. "Are you okay?" she asked. One more nurse arrived, and together, they helped me get back in my bed.

Shortly after, the doctor arrived in a hurry. He asked to see my medication logs. While reading, he looked surprised and kept shaking his head. Then, he gave the chart back to the nurse and gave her some instructions. The doctor ordered that I stay in bed all day, and the nurses were to bring all my meals up to my room during the day.

I was so puzzled. I had no clue why I had collapsed. However, there was one thing I knew for sure: I was deeply affected emotionally.

Later, Mom came to see me. The nurse gave her some explanation. She told her I just had a negative side effect from the medicine, but it was nothing serious. Then, they allowed her to come up into my room.

When I saw her coming, I couldn't help bursting into tears. I asked her why. "Why is all of this happening to me, Mom? Why am I being punished? Why, if I've never hurt anybody?"

My mom remained standing by my side, rigid. She looked pale. She told me I shouldn't despair because everything would pass soon.

"I am so tired. I want all of this to end! I don't think I can continue like this much longer. I'm tired, Mom. I'm tired," I kept saying.

She remained silent for a moment, just staring at me. Then she said, "Yes, you can. You can continue because you are my daughter. You're strong like me. You're perfectly able to overcome all of this. You can, and you will."

Mom's face expressed so much concern. And she failed in her efforts to make her voice sound as strong as her words.

The truth came out the following day when I was able to leave my room and talk to some other patients. They told me they knew why I had collapsed the previous morning. It turned out the doctor on duty that night hadn't increased the dose of the pills I was taking but rather had prescribed a different medicine. A medicine that happened to be way too strong for me. They had overheard the nurses saying the medicine was "strong enough to put a horse to sleep."

WHAT CAME AFTER MY DISCHARGE FROM THE PSYCH HOSPITAL?

I stayed at the hospital for a whole week. At discharge, they prescribed some anxiolytics I should take in case I felt too anxious or nervous.

I went back to work and tried to continue with my life. Nonetheless, my problems hadn't ceased. I kept having trouble staying asleep, and I kept feeling tired. The inability to feel rested made each day difficult to go through. I couldn't be productive at work because I couldn't concentrate. The anxiety kept building. My stay at the hospital didn't help me at all, unfortunately.

"Now, what am I going to do?" I wondered. "What road should I take?" I kept asking myself. I needed to find a way to relieve the tension.

I thought reconnecting with my old friends could help me loosen up. I had high school friends I hadn't seen for a few years.

I started by visiting Yadira, my closest friend at the time. Yadira married very young and had her first child at age eighteen. She led a life so different from mine. She was a stay-at-home mom, and she didn't have the urge to have a job. Her husband, although not a professional, was a hard-working man and provided for his family. They didn't have many financial resources, but they seemed happy.

Yadira welcomed me with a big smile. I could tell she was thrilled.

"Evelyn, darling, it's so nice to see you! We haven't seen each other for such a long time. Have a seat. I'm glad to see you still remember me; you haven't stopped by for so long."

The joy Yadira displayed made me feel at ease.

"Hello, Yadira, my dear friend! How are you doing? Hey, you also know where I live, and yet you haven't visited me for a long time, either."

"Evelyn, I went to see you more than once. They always told me you were out. You are away from home a lot. It would be easier for you to come to see me because I'm almost always home."

"You are right, my dear; I should visit you more often. As a matter of fact, we should contact all the prom girls for a reunion. We can talk and remember anecdotes from our school years."

"Yes, I love the idea. I have the phone numbers of most of the girls. I can contact them. We should plan ahead so most of them can attend. You know, some are busy with college, others with work, and some others, like me, are busy raising their children. But if we pick a date way in advance, I'm pretty sure most of them will show up."

We began to go over some of the funniest anecdotes of our high school years.

"Do you remember, Yadira, the day the math teacher gave us the graded written exam and one of the girls, Martha, I think was her name, got a bad grade? It was five out of twenty, I believe. Then, out of sheer outrage, she tore that paper to pieces. It must've helped her feel better because she kept smiling after doing it. Eventually, the teacher told us to sign the paper and return it. Poor Martha she was trying to put the pieces together like a puzzle. And all of us laughed out loud."

Those were almost magical moments. I had managed to laugh spontaneously. It certainly was a good idea to reconnect with my dear friend.

Yadira said, "Tell me, how are you doing at work? You work in an office, right?"

"That's right, in an office. I'm doing very well; I'm very happy. My work is simple; I must type in documents, hand them out to the other offices, answer the phone, assist in coordinating conferences, etc. The place is beautiful and elegant. When I am there, I feel like I'm not poor." We both laughed.

"And in the evening, I go to school to become a teacher of English."

"I'm glad you're doing so well, darling. I had to stop school when I had my first child. And now that I have two, it is almost impossible to return. My husband works hard, but there's no way he can afford to pay for my school as well. Besides, I don't have anybody to watch my children. But I'd love to work and help my husband with the household expenses. I would also love to have some extra money to spend on whatever I want."

"You are so lucky to have two healthy and beautiful children. Enjoy them. Children grow up fast. When they are bigger, you'll be able to resume your career."

"That's what my husband also tells me, 'Be patient, make sure our children grow up well taken care of; I'll take care of the money.' But the truth is, staying at home every day and doing household chores most of the time isn't very exciting."

I felt like saying, "It would be okay with me to stay home, at least for a couple of months, without worrying about taking care of the money."

"So why don't we switch?" she said. "You come to my house, and I go to your office."

We both laughed out loud once more.

Soon after, my good mood faded away. I wasn't smiling anymore.

"You look worried. Is something wrong?" Yadira asked.

"Nothing serious," I replied. "You know, we all have problems of one kind or another."

I certainly wasn't going to tell her I had spent seven days in a mental hospital. I was pretty sure If I told her, she would start seeing me with different eyes. The problem with my stomach became the central topic of the conversation.

"For several months, I've had serious medical problems with my stomach. I've been getting terrible stomachaches. The pain was so intense I ended up in the ER on a few occasions. But what disturbs me the most is the fact that they have run many exams and blood tests already, but they haven't been able to find the root of the problem."

"That sure is very weird," said Yadira. "If something is wrong, it should appear on the test results." She thought for a moment. "Let me tell you something. Some time ago, my father's arms and legs would swell without any apparent reason. Same as you, they ran tests, but they didn't find anything wrong. Weird stuff started happening around the house. Things would get lost and later show up in a place nobody could have thought of."

Yadira paused. Then, in a mysterious tone, she asked, "Darling, do you believe in witchcraft?"

"I don't know. Why are you asking?"

"Let me continue," she said.

"At the time, we were doing very poorly. My husband couldn't get a job, although he was looking like crazy. At home, there was almost always one of us sick. We were having a very tough time. We could feel a bad vibe around and didn't know what was going on. One day, my mother's midwife recommended that she visit a shaman she knew of. Mom went to see the guy. He told her somebody had hurt us with witchcraft. And for this reason, everything was going wrong for us. The shaman then gave Mom some stuff to do what they call "a cleanse" in my house. After that, everything started to improve for all of us. Maybe this is the case with you, too. There are very bad people in this world, believe me. And since you're doing well, you are advancing academically and financially; envious people may want to harm you and prevent you from progressing."

Witchcraft was something I would never have considered. However, at this point in my distress, I thought I shouldn't leave any stone unturned.

*The Shaman and the ritual

My mom and my sister Melina came with me. I had envisioned a discreet location, but when we arrived at the place, what we found was a conglomeration of people of all ages waiting to see the shaman, including children. I had no idea there was such a demand for this type of service. We had to join the long queue on the street by the door of a kind of corral.

Upon entering, they made us sit on some wooden steps in a large rustic-looking room. The assistant shaman informed us that we had to wait until it started to get dark to begin the ritual.

Two assistant shamans in charge of the organization and maintaining order ensured everyone had paid. Immediately afterward, they distributed some leaves that seemed to be olive.

One of the assistants began by saying, "We are going to use the olive leaves to cleanse our bodies of the bad vibes that keep us captive. Shake the bouquets with energy all over your body. Start at the head and work your way down slowly. You must put all your faith in the healing power of the olive leaves. At the same time, let us ask the almighty to fill us with all the necessary blessings to free us from the evil one."

They started singing songs of praise while all the attendees walked in circles. Another assistant continued, "Now, you all must drink this medicine. It has been made out of holy water."

They handed out small plastic cups containing an opaque liquid. It was a kind of herb water. I just tasted it; it was bitter. I didn't know what it contained, so there was no way I was going to drink it. I put the cup aside. Most of the attendees did drink it completely, without any qualms.

The assistant said, "Now, the companions of the ill person must place their hands on them. Let's close our eyes and pray. Let us ask our creator, Almighty God, to free your bodies and souls of all evil and protect you from the bad energy of all those envious people who don't want to see you succeed. He has promised that if you pray with all the strength of your faith, tonight you will leave this place completely healed! Amen."

There was a pause. The organizers weren't giving any other directions right now, so I took the opportunity to ask the people sitting next to me some questions. There was a married couple and their seven-year-old daughter. They told me the girl was in poor health and the doctors hadn't been able to give her a definite diagnosis. They were looking for alternatives. Apparently, we had something in common. I kept asking questions.

They told me it was the second session they were attending. "And has your child had any improvement?" I asked. "A little bit," the mother replied. "They told us to bring her today because later they would do a different kind of healing ritual for her. They have promised she'll improve in a few more sessions."

Then, the assistants signaled for everyone to go silent. The head shaman then appeared and began to lead the session.

"Each person who is here looking for healing, along with your family members, will have to approach the center of the room. Then, walk slowly toward the opening in the roof until you are standing exactly under the moonlight. The accompanying group must pay close attention; you must concentrate. When your family member is in the right place, you'll be able to see the silhouette of the person responsible for the witchcraft. Again, you must focus."

The first group approached. They did exactly as the shaman had told them. The shaman then asked if they had seen the silhouette. They mentioned someone. Each group was free to reveal the name of the person they were seeing or keep it secret.

Something fishy happened with one of the groups, an anecdote I still remember after so long. When one of the clients was standing right under the moonlight, the head shaman said out loud, "Concentrate, concentrate, you're about to know who that person is. Can you see it? Do you know who it is?"

A lady in the group whispered a name, but she sounded unsure. "Ca – Carlos," she said quietly.

The head shaman took advantage of the opportunity and yelled, "If the name starts with the letter C, that's the person!"

To which the other members of the group responded aloud, "Carlos, Carlos!"

Everybody was positive that they had seen the silhouettes, but not everyone revealed the names. My turn had come. My mom and sister stood with me. We also did as everyone else had so far. Mom said she saw a silhouette, too. But she didn't mention the name.

The next morning, I asked my mom whose silhouette she had seen that night.

"Nobody's, darling," she answered. "I didn't tell you before because I didn't want to take away your hope that we would make a discovery. I'm sorry, honey."

"Don't worry, Mom. We always learn something, even from the most absurd things."

Regarding this anecdote, there's a question that will always remain unanswered and has kept me intrigued for decades ...What could have possibly happened to that guy, Carlos?

CAN MDD BE EASILY OBSERVED BY OTHERS?

One true thing about depression, the disease, is the fact that others can't observe it. If we don't want them to notice there's something wrong with us, we can conceal it, even when we are feeling dreadful.

One Saturday morning, my older brother, Ernesto, came to visit. Apparently, Mom had told him something about my health problem. First, he and Mom spent a long time talking. I was in my room completely disheveled, still in pajamas, even though it was almost noon time. I didn't have the energy to shower or even comb my hair. Just thinking about having to do all of this made me tired.

But I knew that before leaving, Ernesto was going to ask to speak with me, and this was causing me lots of anxiety. I couldn't allow him to see me in that awful state. Even in my worst times, I was still proud. My appearance was visual evidence that I wasn't in control. I felt embarrassed. I needed to force myself into changing my clothes, doing my hair, and putting a little makeup on.

Accomplishing these small tasks was a challenge. It felt like I was trying to drive a car, but trying to push it was all I could do.

My brother and I talked. He tried to give me some advice. "That problem with nerves happens to all of us. It's very common. At my work, for example, there's always a lot of tension. We have a lot of money in our care, and there's always the risk of being mugged or even killed. I have sometimes felt a lot of anxiety while doing my job. But I immediately shake off all those fears, those bad thoughts, put a smile on my face, and I **just snap out of it**! You can do the same. You just need to get rid of the negative thoughts, that's all."

"Sure," I replied, trying to sound as normal as possible. I kept a straight posture, and I managed to keep the conversation flowing without showing any sign of distress.

"As you say, it's all on me. I'm aware of that. But Mom is exaggerating things; I just have exhaustion. I work and go to school at the same time, you know. All I need is a few days off and some rest."

"Yeah, you look good, so I guess it isn't anything serious...."

"I'm telling you, it isn't."

Ernesto finally left.

If I hadn't been seated, I would've fallen on the floor. I felt dead.

At that moment, Mom arrives and says, "Evelyn, you look very good! You even put some makeup on. I can see you feel better! There's no doubt your brother's visit was beneficial for you. I'm going to ask him to come over more often."

From a 16-year-old girl's post on the Internet. Elise J.:

"I want you to picture a person with depression. Are you seeing the dark bedroom, filthy sweatpants, empty eyes, poor health, and general lack of prosperity? Do you know what I see? A blonde, blue-eyed teenage girl. She gets awesome grades, loves Instagram, loves to paint, goes to football games, drinks Starbucks, and giggles with her friends. She can quote Harry Potter, obsesses over makeup tutorials, and cannot wait for college. She looks back at me every morning in the mirror."

CHAPTER 3

IDENTIFYING THE EMOTIONAL STRUGGLE AS SEPARATE FROM THE PHYSICAL DISEASE

To finally end the constant swapping of concepts, we need to establish clear boundaries between plain emotional issues and those resulting from abnormal biological changes. While working on this task, I labeled them with the following classifications:

The non-disease depression is **PSYCHOEMOTIONAL DEPRESSION.**

The physical disease is **STRESS-DRIVEN NEUROBIOLOGICAL ILLNESS (SDNBI)** as a substitute for major depressive disorder.

A.- PSYCHOLOGICAL/EMOTIONAL DEPRESSION

This is the depression most people talk about. We all experience it at one point or another in our lives. It varies in seriousness and length. Some people can experience mild depression, others a more serious one. It isn't a disease. Instead, it's an emotional health issue.

In this scenario, since most people have reasons for their emotional despair, they must concentrate on finding solutions for those reasons. The next step would be to modify negative thoughts and unhealthy attitudes. The following step would be to make necessary changes in their lifestyle.

Characteristics

1.- It is about broken hearts.

2.-The adjective "depressed" is consistent with the state of mind (sadness, low mood).

3.- Called 'reactive' depression because it follows an adverse event.

4.- The depressed person can identify what is troubling them. For example, the death of a loved one, a divorce, etc.

5.- It remits when the stressor is gone, the problem is resolved, or the troubled person adapts to his/her new reality.

6.- It is the modern epidemic. The rate of depression has been on the rise for decades. Some say it may be due to the present lifestyle; it's too demanding. Everybody is on the run these days, people are losing interpersonal connections, and many interact with machines more than with other human beings.

7.- Medication is not recommended. There's no need for pills; we need to learn skills.

If in a crisis, benzodiazepines might be prescribed by your physician. Benzos are not antidepressants; they are actually the opposite. They are central nervous system depressants. They produce sedation to relieve anxiety and muscle spasms. Among the most prescribed benzos are Valium, Xanax, Halcion, Ativan, Klonopin, Diazepam, Clonazepam, and Lorazepam. They are not intended for long-term use because they can cause addiction. I'm including this information because I have heard some people say, "Antidepressants don't solve your health problem; they just numb you." I can say that this statement is incorrect. Antidepressants don't numb you; "depressants" do.

8. A psychologist or a psychotherapist may help with talk therapy. Cognitive Behavioral Therapy (CBT) is the most used these days. It is based on the idea that the person is having difficulties because of faulty thinking and behaviors.

9. Taking in more sunlight is a natural antidepressant. Lightboxes are also on the market. I've never tried one, but some people say they are helpful.

10.- Exercising can help lift the mood.

Many people have different opinions on how we should handle depression. There are "step programs" online to beat depression. You may take one of them. There are similar books you could buy too. Also, if you are depressed because you feel lonely, dare to go and find someone. I met my husband through a dating site. He happened to be an outstanding human being. He's my hero; I couldn't be more pleased to have him as my life partner (always be cautious, however).

There's no better or worse method, but there is the one that works for you. Let's always remember that although we are similar, we also have our unique side. Offering a one-size-fits-all solution is rarely the best approach.

Other factors that can result in emotional depression:

I.- Grief

Grief is the psychological-emotional anguish experienced after a significant loss. It encompasses <u>any kind of loss.</u>

1.- The loss of a loved one by death (bereavement)

2.- The loss of a parent at an early age, especially the mother, either by death or abandonment.

3.- Divorce (loss of a marriage)

4.- Loss of a friendship

5.- Loss of a job

6.- Illness (loss of your health)

7.- Loss of money (or loss of income)

8.- Incarceration (loss of freedom)

9.- Loss of a dream

10.- Loss of hope

11.- Loss of connections (moving far away from your current community)

12.- Loss of reputation

13. Loss of life purpose

14. Loss of youth and good looks

II.- Emotional burdens

1.- Frustration

2.- Anger

3.-Fear

4.- Loneliness (When we wish we had someone, not when we are alone by choice)

5.- Trauma

6.- Jealousy

7.- Resentment

8.- Guilt

9.- Failure

10.-Embarrassment

11.-Low self-esteem

12.- Rejection (e.g., someone feeling not accepted for their sexual orientation).

III.- Social and Environmental Factors

1.- Bullying

2.- Financial issues

3.- Burdensome relationships

4.- Poverty

5.- Disability

6.- Exposure to violence

7.- Abandonment/neglect

8.- Abuse (physical and sexual molestation)

9.- Being a migrant or refugee

10.- Racism

11.- Stressful job environment

12.- Lack of proper housing

13.- Lack of health insurance

14.- Lack of good-paying jobs

15.- Lack of justice

16.- Lack of sleep

17.- Lack of physical exercise

B.- STRESS-DRIVEN NEUROBIOLOGICAL ILLNESS (SDNBI)

This section of the book is of particular interest to people who are going or have gone through a serious case of the disease. To those who have received successful treatment, to patients with treatment-resistant MDD, and to all the families this ailment has touched. You are the group of people who can identify with this information and understand it better.

I respectfully suggest everybody else be cautious and refrain from expressing an opinion about this disease you do not know about personally. This kind of experience, in particular, cannot be created; we just undergo it.

Since this concerns a medical condition, you should discuss it with your physician. And you should look for support from people with the same challenges. Those who are going through the same struggle can understand us better than anyone else, and we can certainly support each other.

Not having more appropriate words to talk about this disease makes it challenging to express its actual meaning. Therefore, I have created some new nomenclatures for this purpose.

* **SDNBI** replacing MDD, clinical, or unipolar depression

* **SDNBI patients** instead of depressed patients

* **BRAIN RESTORATIVE MEDICINES (BRM)** as a substitute for antidepressants

* **PEOPLE SUFFERING FROM SDNBI** instead of people who are depressed

Characteristics

1.- It's about broken brains, not broken hearts.

Several interlocked determinants influence the way our brains develop, adapt, and respond to stress from conception throughout life.

2.- It falls into the category of uncontrollable. Uncontrollable is the hallmark of the disease.

3.- Many people have a rhythmic pattern to the disease that is controlled by their biological clock. This means they can get sick at a certain age, every certain number of years, or during wintertime only.

4.- It is heritable. Genes are passed on from the parents to the offspring. Studies with twins and adoption studies have indicated that genetic factors often play an essential role in the development of SDNBI.

5.- This disease usually goes hand in hand with generalized anxiety disorder.

Repeat bouts of anxiety signal elevated levels of stress. Chronic stress usually leads to the expression of this stress-sensitive disease.

6.- It can occur **with** external precipitants. People with a genetic predisposition are more likely to develop the disease after experiencing a traumatic event.

7.- It can occur **without** external triggers or precipitants. Affected people can't easily identify the main reason for their despair (because diseases have causes instead of reasons to be). Many even express that they have a good life.

"...my dank joylessness was, therefore, all the more ironic because I had flown on a rushed four-day trip to Paris in order to accept an award that should have sparklingly restored my ego."

WILLIAM STYRON

Darkness Visible

"To be depressed when you have experienced trauma or when your life is clearly a mess is one thing, but to sit around and be depressed when you are finally at a remove from trauma, and your life is not a mess is awfully confusing and destabilizing."

ANDREW SOLOMON

The Noonday Demon

"...I have had few real difficulties. I have had, on the contrary, an exceptionally glamorous life—as lives go... But, since my childhood, I have suffered from melancholia... It has prevented my getting anything like the full value out of my talents, and, for the past three years, has made work a torture to do at all...."

RALPH BARTON

An excerpt from his Suicide Note

8.- Medical treatment is recommended. To cure the disease, we need pills. To prevent relapse, we need skills.

I have read about people who received psychotherapy for a long time. They said they felt therapy had helped them well enough to keep going. But it wasn't until they got medical treatment that they realized they had been living only half-life. Never before had they felt life could be so effortless. Only after successful medical treatment could these people enjoy life to the fullest.

9.- Ideally, it should be a psychiatrist or a neuropsychiatrist who treats the patient.

Most physicians have a license to prescribe BRMs. However, this complex disease should be treated by highly trained and experienced specialists in these medical fields.

10.- It's more prevalent among women (for every two women, one man develops the disease).

Hormonal fluctuations in women may be one of the triggers.

11. Symptoms usually start showing up early in life and are also very prevalent during young adulthood.

Other factors that can contribute to SDNBI

1.- Prenatal events may influence gene expression (they turn on and off).

a.- When the mother undergoes too much stress during pregnancy, like in every stress response, the body secretes distinct kinds of stress hormones, like adrenaline and cortisol. Too much cortisol is like poison to the brain.

b.- Pregnant women who smoke and consume alcohol or recreational drugs may give birth to children with all kinds of problems, including damage to the central nervous system.

c.- When the mother doesn't follow a healthy diet, this can also cause a negative impact on the development of the brain and nervous system.

2.- Hypothyroidism

3.- Significant hormonal changes (e.g., postpartum depression)

4.- Serious food allergies can directly disrupt brain functions

5.- Poor nutrition (junk and inflammatory foods like soy, corn, gluten, vegetable oil, excess sugar, high fructose syrup, lack of healthy fats, etc.)

6.- Certain vitamin deficiencies (Bs and Ds)

7.- Anemia

8.- Certain medications (prescribed and even OTC)

9.- Brain poisoning (lead, fumes, insecticides, smoke, harsh chemicals, etc.)

10.- Concussions (Caused by accidents or while playing rough sports. It may have happened long before, and you may not even remember about it)

11.- Brain tumors

12.- Inflammation in the brain (Unremitting stress can induce an inflammatory response of the immune system)

13.- Infectious diseases (Lyme disease, hepatitis C)

14.- Issues in the gut (the brain and the gastrointestinal system are intimately connected. An imbalanced microbiome in the gut can affect brain health. Likewise, a troubled brain can cause stomach problems)

15.- STD (HIV, Syphilis)

16.- Immune System Diseases (e.g., multiple sclerosis, lupus)

17.- Diabetes

18.- Obesity

19.- Drug addiction

20.- Alcoholism

I suggest watching the following YouTube videos:

*THE SURPRISINGLY DRAMATIC ROLE OF NUTRITION IN MENTAL HEALTH.

Julia Rucklidge, clinical psychologist, 2014.

*SCIENTISTS INVESTIGATE THE LINK BETWEEN DEPRESSION AND GUT BACTERIA.

ITV News. 2019.

CHAPTER 4

GOING OVER THE SCIENTIFIC EVIDENCE

THE BRAIN AT A GLANCE

I want to start by reviewing some basics about the brain. Let's begin by taking a glance at the functions of a healthy brain:

The human brain is the most outstanding, unique, complex, and, so far, impossible-to-replicate machine known to humankind. If we had the fastest and most advanced computer in our heads instead of a brain, we wouldn't be able to function as human beings at all.

We have around 100 billion neurons, also called nerve cells or brain cells. There are three main kinds of neurons; different types perform different activities:

SENSORY NEURONS. – Perceive light, smell, sound, taste, heat, and pressure. For us to be able to see images, smell odors, taste flavors, hear noise, touch, and feel, we need our sensory neurons to be working fine.

MOTOR NEURONS. – For us to be able to perform any movement, these neurons must first transmit messages from the brain out to the motor control and to the muscles. When we stand up and walk, our motor neurons are at work.

INTERNEURONS. – They connect all other neurons. They do not contact the external environment.

Neurons form clusters or networks. Each neuron carries information that passes on to another neuron and then to another, like a chain. The brain sends and receives "chemical and electrical" signals throughout the body. Different signals control different processes, and the brain interprets each. Some make you feel tired, while others make you feel pain. Some messages are kept within the brain, while others are relayed through the spine and across the body's network of nerves to distant extremities. To do this, the central nervous system (CNS) relies on billions of neurons in its entire system.

The nervous system has two main parts: The Central Nervous System, which is made up of the brain and the spinal cord, and the peripheral nervous system, which is made up of nerves that branch off from the spinal cord and extend to all parts of the body. The Nervous System receives and sends messages between the brain and the rest of the body, including internal organs.

For the brain to communicate with the rest of the body and to function in an optimal way, all the elements that play a role in the brain cell communication processes must be in optimal condition and working properly.

Among the aspects to consider are the brain structure, circuits, neural connections (synapses), chemistry composition (hormones, neurotransmitters), electrical signals, blood flow, and oxygen level (among many other possibilities considering its profound complexity). If there happen to be any negative alterations, it may bring all this organized, symphony-like tuning of the brain out of synchronicity, which then will be expressed by producing symptoms that will make us feel ill.

WHERE DO OUR FEELINGS AND EMOTIONS COME FROM?

I grew up hearing that love comes from the heart. Is it true?

The brain is involved in virtually everything we do. It is the headquarters where every single thought, feeling, emotion, and decision is processed along with all our senses and movements.

Our brain determines our personality, controls our cognitive abilities, memory, concentration, intelligence, speech, and perception, and controls our vision. With our brain, we love, hate, suffer, learn, feel pleasure, feel pain, and feel hungry. It makes us sleepy, and we use it for everything else we do or think about.

Do we breathe with our brains, too?

We sure do! In the lower part of our brain is something called the brain stem. It connects the upper brain with the spinal cord.

Basic bodily activities for our survival are regulated by the brain stem, such as breathing, heart rhythm, circulation, oxygen levels, swallowing, digestion, and so much more. If this part of the brain got damaged, what do you think would happen?

The brain has the greatest power over us. Since it is connected to every single part of the body via the nervous system, the consequences of any structural alterations or faulty functions are acknowledged by all other parts of the body. The loss of brain-function synchronicity can be expressed through an array of serious, intense, relentless, and even incapacitating multi-organ physical symptoms that can compromise our emotions, too. Consequently, SDNBI ends up being not only an illness of the brain and the nervous system but also an illness of the whole body! This is exactly why, when it is out of control, it is one of the most ruthless diseases one can have.

DO BRAINS AFFECTED BY SDNBI LOOK AND FUNCTION DIFFERENTLY?

According to research in psychiatry, neurology, and other related fields, there's substantial evidence that brains with SDNBI have structural abnormalities, as well as functional differences, compared to healthy brains.

Advances in functional neuroimaging over the past 25 years have provided powerful tools for advancing brain science. They have revolutionized the field of psychiatry in particular.

So far, the only thing that has separated psychiatric disorders from neurologic disorders has been the inability to find neuropathology. Because of this, the ability to visualize and quantify brain structure and function noninvasively in living people is particularly important for psychiatric illnesses. It can make it possible to associate mental disorders with abnormal biology.

In fact, contemporary psychiatric neuroimaging techniques have permitted a more advanced understanding of brain circuit abnormalities in psychiatric diseases. This, in combination with progress in basic neuroscience, has laid a foundation for medical progress. Neural circuit dysfunction associated with psychiatric syndromes can be localized.

A number of fundamental findings were produced with these methods (you don't have to understand all this information thoroughly, but you can get a general idea of the physical causes of SDNBI). For example:

a.- under-activity of the frontal lobes (the front part of the brain)

It seems an underactive prefrontal cortex produces low motivation, low appetite, and a lack of hope.

b.- Over-activity in the amygdala and the hypothalamic-pituitary-adrenal [HPA] axis

An overactive "amygdala" produces insomnia, anxiety, and suicidal tendencies.

Nonetheless, due to the complexity of the brain, it's more possible that the dysfunction among the interaction of multiple areas in the brain causes the issues.

What is the amygdala?

The amygdala is an almond-shaped structure located deep inside the brain. It's part of the limbic system (a group of structures associated with emotions such as fear, anger, pleasure, sorrow, and sexual arousal). We could say the amygdala represents the alarm system in the brain because it is activated every time we perceive a threat. The amygdala plays an important role in the "fight or flight" response (Fast breathing, accelerated heart rate, muscle tension, nervousness, sweat). This stress response can happen even when we are just recalling a frightening situation.

The combination of a hyperactive amygdala and an underactive pre-frontal cortex is likely to be involved in anxiety disorders. People with a damaged amygdala show impaired fear conditioning. Individuals with this characteristic have a reduced ability to extinguish fear and control anxiety. Their rational thinking can't tame the emotional reaction. It means although they understand there's no reason to get anxious because the perceived threat is not real or is under control, they can't help feeling anxious anyway.

* Stress vs. Anxiety

Stress is the psycho-physiological response to internal or external stressors. Stress involves changes affecting nearly every system of the body and may manifest with an accelerated heart rate, sweating, muscle tone, shortness of breath, dry mouth, fidgeting, fast speech, etc. Stress can affect our health, contributing directly to diseases. People under stress can also experience changes in their sleep patterns, fatigue, irritability, digestive problems, and muscle pain. Anxiety, however, is defined by excessive worry that persists even after the stressor is gone.

c.- Dysfunction of the nucleus accumbent

What is the nucleus accumbent?

The NAc is a key structure in mediating emotional and motivational processing. Pleasure, the drive for rewards (such as food, sex, fame, and buying new stuff...), is mediated through the NAc with input from a variety of other structures. People with SDNBI are suspected of having a dysfunctional NAc. This can explain why they have Anhedonia, the inability to feel pleasure. It has been possible to identify the reward system in certain brain regions.

*A study about the reward system in the brain

In 1954, James Olds and Peter Milner reported evidence for the existence of a reward center.

They implanted an electrode through the skull into the brain of a rat. The rat was placed in a box containing a lever. When the rat pressed the lever, it received a mild stimulus- which can be highly motivating. Depending on where the electrode was placed, the rats would press the lever up to 5000 times in an hour! They would not stop even to eat. They chose brain stimulation over food. The rats would keep doing it until they died.

This may mean that if they conducted the same experiment with humans, they could make us experience pleasure and feel extremely happy just by stimulating specific areas of the brain. It would also mean that if the same brain areas were underactive, it could make us feel sad and unable to experience pleasure.

At present, there is a similar practice called deep brain stimulation. DBS consists of placing electrodes deep in the brain to modulate and correct neural circuitry abnormalities. It is like a pacemaker for the brain. DBS is a procedure aimed at helping patients who have not responded to other treatments for SDNBI (treatment-resistant depression). As we can see, the brain can be manipulated and even changed with externally applied electricity because the brain is an electrical organ.

In a TED Talk, Dr. Helen Mayberg, a neurologist and pioneer on DBS, reports her findings when working with seriously ill patients who had tried hard to beat the disease, but nothing had worked for them. Some of her quotes include, "DBS doesn't make it easy – it makes it possible." "DBS doesn't push positive – it enables positive." "It helps you jump out."

d.- A bigger number of neurons in the hypothalamus:

Post-mortem findings help define disorders more clearly by their demonstrable pathology in the brain. Postmortem analyses of patients who had depression show an overpopulation of neurons. Too many neurons in this area make the Hypothalamic Pituitary Adrenal Axis hyperactive. The reason for having a bigger number of neurons in this area is believed to be genetic or the result of chronic stress. Ongoing stress can cause the HPA axis to be unable to self-regulate.

What is the Hypothalamus?

The hypothalamus sits in a commanding position within the central nervous system (CNS). It is located above the pituitary gland. The hypothalamus regulates body temperature, controls hunger and thirst, and plays a role in some aspects of memory and emotion.

We all have an internal clock that controls the daily ups and downs of biological patterns. The hypothalamus is involved in circadian (about a day) rhythms or sleep-wake cycles. Research suggests that an out-of-sync internal clock may be a factor in depression and related disorders.

e.- A Smaller Hippocampus:

What is the Hippocampus?

The hippocampus is a folded structure incorporated within the temporal lobe. It plays an essential role in the development of long-term memories, learning, navigation, and perception of space. Possibly, some people are born with a smaller hippocampus. Nonetheless, researchers believe the excess stress hormone cortisol may be what causes this brain area to shrink.

f.- Smaller Pre-Frontal Cortex, Cingulate Gyrus, and Cerebellum.

What is the Pre-frontal Cortex?

The prefrontal cortex is the area of the brain above the eyebrows beneath the forehead. The cortex refers to the dense outer layer covering the upper part of the brain called the cerebrum. The cerebral cortex comprises gray matter. Gray matter is primarily composed of neuron somas (the round central cell bodies). The white matter is made of axons (the parts of the neuron that branch off the cell body and look like long stems that connect brain cells together). The gray matter is on the outside, and the white matter sits within.

The prefrontal cortex is the most evolved part of the brain, the headquarters where the executive orders take place. It subserves our highest-order cognitive abilities. Nonetheless, this brain region is the most sensitive to stress, too. Without the prefrontal cortex, we wouldn't be able to reason and control our behavior, nor could we solve problems or plan ahead.

g.- Decreased cortical thickness

Substantial thinning of the cerebral cortex has been demonstrated in a number of neurological and psychiatric conditions like depression, dementia, schizophrenia, and neurodegenerative disorders.

h.- Diminished neural size (smaller brain cells).

Premature shrinkage of the brain cells is possibly due to excess of the stress hormone cortisol. Nonetheless, it's normal for the brain to begin to shrink between the ages of 30 and 40.

i.-Decreased level of Brain-Derived Neurotrophic Factor Protein (BDNF).

Like the alarm system and the internal clock, the brain has a maintenance system, too. It uses immature stem cells for this purpose. The stem cells migrate to any part of the brain where they are needed, either to repair or grow more nerve cells. When these cells mature, they become the new, younger cells needed to maintain the brain in optimal condition. This system is called neurogenesis.

Factor proteins are needed for the process of neurogenesis. It seems the levels of BDNF protein in people with clinical depression are low. Not having enough of this protein disrupts the process of neurogenesis, and poor stimulation of nerve growth happens, which then causes loss of neural volume and shrinkage of the brain. Postmortem analyses of suicide subjects found a marked decrease in this protein in their prefrontal cortex and hippocampus.

Apart from all the suggested evidence listed, there may be other factors for this malady. With 100 billion neurons, 100 trillion neural connections, and thousands of chemical and electrical reactions per second in our brains, it would be an arduous task to identify what exactly is failing in each patient's brain. But what we know is that there is usually something wrong with the nervous system of people suffering from SDNBI.

CHAPTER 5

ALL ABOUT THE MEDICAL TREATMENT FOR MY SDNB

BEING TREATABLE DOESN'T MAKE IT SIMPLE

Some people think that because unipolar depression is treatable, it's not a big deal. The wicked truth about this disease is that there's no treatment that can provide prompt and safe relief from the excruciating physical symptoms. And finding the right medicine for everyone can be a challenge. Treatment starts with trial and error. If a particular medication isn't working for you, the psychiatrist will change it to another one. If that doesn't help either, they will change medication again, and so on. Furthermore, a patient may not respond to any type of BRM (antidepressant) by itself, so then it is time to combine two different medications, and so on. It can turn into a long, agonizing process.

Some may be lucky and find the matching medicine right away. Others will have to keep on trying for several weeks or even months. In the meantime, the patient continues enduring this sort of piercing toothache. No relief, although he/she is taking medication and seeing the doctor every week. Furthermore, every time the dose is adjusted or the medicine is changed, it feels like one more tooth begins to hurt, and the excruciating pain intensifies the following week and the one that follows, and so on. We can be at the mercy of the disease and the side effects of the medications for quite some time, and they will show no compassion.

MEETING THE NEW PSYCHIATRIST

My quest to find out where my health issues were coming from continued. At this point, I realized I definitely couldn't continue working in such poor health. I asked for a leave of absence, and they agreed to it.

Through one of her friends, my mom met a nurse who knew an outstanding psychiatrist. This nurse worked at the same clinic Dr. E. worked at. She told Mom she was positive this doctor was one of the best psychiatrists in the capital city of Lima, and there weren't many as qualified as he was.

It sounded like a ray of hope to me. Nonetheless, not everything was good news. Although I had health insurance through my job, under this government-run system, I couldn't choose doctors. If I was going to start treatment with a doctor who wasn't in their program, the insurance wouldn't cover the charges, not even the medications he would prescribe.

So, if this doctor was one of the best psychiatrists in Lima-Perú, it also meant seeing him would be very expensive. I was aiming for high-end-quality medical treatment, so I would have to cover all the expenses out of pocket. I was afraid this could be something I wouldn't be able to pay for.

We went to see him anyway. While we were in the waiting room, many things were going through my head, "Will this doctor be able to help me? How? What if there's definitely nothing doctors can do to help me? What if, as I hear constantly, it all depends on me, and only I can help myself?

Heaven knows I just can't!

Finally, the office door opened. I saw this friendly-looking man approaching. He must've been in his mid-forties with short hair sprinkled with gray and wearing a white doctor's gown.

He greeted us with a smile and shook hands with Mom and me.

"Good afternoon. Go ahead, have a seat."

My mom responded, "Good afternoon, doctor. Thank you for giving us the appointment promptly.

"Nurse Sandra told me about you," said the doctor. "What is your name?"

"Evelyn," I responded with a forced smile.

The psychiatrist asked me all the questions I had been asked before and more. I guess he was trying to get to know me in many aspects of my personality. And, of course, about my current health status.

My mom intervened. "Doctor, Evelyn is a very responsible young lady. She works during the day and goes to school in the evening, which is fine, but I keep telling her she needs to take time to have some fun, too. Everything can't be work-school and more work-school. I think she takes everything too seriously."

"Madam, there are many young people who work and go to school, like your daughter. However, they don't develop depression."

He looked at me and continued. "Let me ask you, has anybody else suffered from depression in your family?"

I responded, "Yes, an older sister got sick with depression a few years ago."

Then he turned to my mom. "Do you know what medicines she was given?"

"I don't remember. It has been long since it happened."

"Could you find out? Because among relatives, the same kind of medication usually works."

"I lost track of the doctor. I think someone told me he had moved abroad."

"That's a pity. It would really help if we had that information.

Now, Evelyn, what do you think has contributed to the development of your depression? Work, school, not having friends, or lack of leisure activities as your mom suggests?"

"Getting this job is the best thing that has ever happened to me. Having a job makes it possible for me to pay for my school. In addition, the environment at work is a lot of fun. I have met a group of girls around my age, and we have developed a strong friendship. I used to go out with them often, but as my health problems were getting more regular, I hadn't felt like going anywhere. Recently, I even broke up with my boyfriend. I felt it wasn't the right time to be in a relationship with anybody."

I paused for a few seconds and then continued. "I must admit, though, I am kind of anxious by nature. I usually find myself fighting these feelings of urgency. I find myself feeling I should be doing more things and faster. But lately, my health issues have been causing me the most anxiety ever. I have had a series of episodes of terrible stomachaches that ended up in the ER several times. I have been going from doctor to doctor and having test after test performed, but they all came out negative. This frustration has been making my muscles tense and my sleep irregular. My energy levels have been dropping steadily. At present, I usually feel sluggish or as if I were getting lazy."

"It can't be laziness, doctor," Mom intervened. "She's always been very active. She likes cleanliness and keeping things in order. Moreover, since she was very young, Evelyn has been willing to work.

Evelyn, how old were you when you started babysitting?" Mom asked.

"I was about fourteen, I think."

"I never forced you to do it; you decided it yourself."

"I knew you didn't have the money to buy everything I needed for my school year. So, I needed to make some money myself."

"I see," said the doctor. "Now, Evelyn, you were hospitalized for seven days some weeks ago, right?"

"Yes, that's right. But it didn't make a difference. I feel even worse now."

"What other issues do you think may have triggered your depression."

"The truth is nothing terrible has happened to me. No member of my family has died recently, I haven't been abused, I have always had my mom by my side, and although I don't live with my father, I have a good relationship with him. I don't see myself as a traumatized human being."

I thought for a moment and then said, "However, the problems with my digestive system have brought me down emotionally, too. You see, I can't eat what I like. I watch everybody else at home eat and enjoy the delicious meals Mom prepares while I must eat soup and Jell-O. And this hasn't been happening just for a short period of time; it's recurring. This may sound silly, but in those moments, I feel excluded. I feel like the ugly duckling."

"I sympathize with you. I would feel terrible if I couldn't eat what I love," Dr. E. commented. "In conclusion, you still don't know what is causing the stomachaches?"

"No. I even had a colonoscopy done, but again, they couldn't find anything wrong. Doctors told me it may be due to stress or anxiety only. Nothing physical."

(Four more years passed before I could demonstrate that I wasn't imagining my stomachaches. Doctors finally found out what was causing them. I will be talking about it later).

"I see. Now, tell me about those days when you were in the hospital. Do you know what medicines they gave you?" Dr. E. asked.

Fortunately, I always asked the nurses what they were giving me, and I wrote it down. So, I handed the doctor my notes.

After reading the paper, the doctor said, "All these medications listed here are basically the same drug but by different names. They're all benzodiazepines, tranquilizers. They are just palliatives, not real medicines."

I was confused, "Not real medicines?"

"I mean, they don't cure any diseases. Evelyn, what you need is real medicine because you ARE sick. Your problem isn't in your mind as you have been told. It's in your body."

The doctor continued, "I have two pieces of news for you, a good one and a bad one. Which do you want to know first?"

"The good one, I guess."

"The good news is there is treatment for your illness, and you can get cured. The bad news is that the treatment is complex. In the beginning, the medicines can cause side effects that can make you feel even worse before you start feeling better."

"I can't even imagine feeling worse than I do right now!" I was sincere when I said this. "And again, more medicine!"

"No, you aren't going to take more medicine. You're going to start taking real medicine. You need to start treatment to cure your illness and not just calm the symptoms temporarily. To start with, I'm going to need commitment on your part."

I was hesitant. "How long will this treatment take, doctor?"

"Between four and six weeks."

"That much time!? I don't feel I could endure one more day feeling like I do now."

"Sorry, there are no shortcuts. We must go all the way. Are you willing to make one more big effort to regain your health?"

"I'm willing to do anything, but where am I going to get the strength I need? Are you sure this treatment will cure me, doctor? What if it doesn't work? It wouldn't have been worth the effort."

"If you follow my instructions closely, the chances are really good that you will be cured."

"Really? Can you promise?"

"I promise," he said with confidence.

I remained silent. I was scared.

Trying to reassure me, Dr. E. added, "Listen, I'm not lying to you; I have already told you it isn't going to be easy. We're going to have to try using more than one kind of antidepressant. But my experience tells me they'll work for you. I promise I'm not going to leave you until you are cured. If I don't end up healing you, I authorize you to come and yell at me as much as you want. I even give you permission to slap me if I don't keep my promise."

He looked closely at me. "Will you be brave and take the challenge?"

The confidence the doctor spoke with became the crutch my soul needed. I had finally found someone who understood I was sick, not just emotionally troubled. This doctor seemed very knowledgeable about my condition. Dr. E. gave me hope.

"Let's get to work then. I'm going to give you the prescription together with the instructions on how you should take the medicines. Ma'am, (the doctor addressed my mom) someone must oversee administering her medications. She herself won't be able to."

"Don't worry, doctor. I'll personally make sure she takes the medicines according to your instructions."

"Evelyn, I need to tell you that upon starting the treatment, you're going to feel quite sore, as if a batch of golf clubs had beaten you up. That's normal, so don't panic. Things are going to be tough, but if you persevere, we'll defeat your disease."

I left the doctor's office carrying with me his promise and my promise to be brave. I had no clue I had agreed to a voyage through an inferno.

*The truth about antidepressant medicines

Below, you will learn about my first encounters with antidepressant medicines. I experienced firsthand the way they actually work. I personally learned that the perception of this kind of medicine is twisted. You may have heard something like, "Antidepressants are happy pills."

People who are ill with MDD don't experience anything even close to happiness after taking antidepressants. I wish it was like that. The shocking truth about these medications is the fact that at the beginning of treatment, they may even worsen the symptoms, especially in young people and those with severe cases. Things can go from bad to unbearable. Some may exacerbate symptoms to an extreme that not many people can tolerate. For this reason, the labels on the containers of this kind of medicine come with a warning for the parents or relatives to be alert because the risk of suicide increases at the beginning of treatment and every time the medication is adjusted or changed.

I have also heard something like, "Just take the medication; what do you have to lose?"

Although medicine of this kind can cure this terrible disease, I have to admit that some of the side effects are insufferable. Because of these horrifying side effects, many people stop taking these medicines and never want to try any other kind of antidepressant.

[Nonetheless, if we pay attention to some commercials for antidepressants, they seem to be selling the idea that they act like magic. As if we started taking them today, by tomorrow, we would feel happy and as fresh as a cucumber. This certainly isn't the case with seriously ill people, so this is deceiving!].

THE COURSE OF TREATMENT

FIRST WEEK

The doctor had prescribed two different kinds of medications. I took the first dose and lay down on my bed. Within a few minutes, I began to feel hot, thick liquid invading my veins and spreading throughout my body. My body temperature rose progressively, and my heart rate accelerated more and more. I could hear my heartbeat as if I had my ears over my chest. I started having trouble breathing. I was gasping for air, and I had to sit up to ease my breathing. Then I felt dizzy and had to lie back down on the bed. I felt my limbs stiffen as if they were made of sticks. I became rigid, wide-eyed, staring at the ceiling. I didn't feel I could move. I felt like I was frozen. I started shivering, but I couldn't even move my arm to reach for my blanket and cover myself up. And in this state of inertia, I remained all night.

The next morning, Mom brought me breakfast in bed.

"Good morning, darling. How are you feeling?"

I didn't want my mom to worry even more, so I simply replied, "So-so, Mom."

"Have your breakfast first so I can give you your medicine."

After taking the second dose of the medicine, I felt the same hot, thick liquid again invading my bloodstream. I was feeling so warm. Again, my body stiffened, and I had to lie back on the bed. I closed my eyes and tried to calm down, but it was useless. I felt worse second by second. Then, I clearly felt like a large, heavy rock had fallen on my chest. I could feel its weight; it was obstructing airflow into my lungs. I needed to sit up to breathe, but the heavyweight sensation didn't allow me to move. My survival instinct made me tilt my head back to position my chin pointing at the ceiling so I wouldn't suffocate. In that position, almost inert, half breathing, and in panic, I had to stay for long hours.

At lunchtime, Mom came into the room again. "Evelyn, here's your lunch. How do you feel?"

Revealing to my mom how bad I was feeling would only make things worse. I knew her blood pressure rose every time she faced difficulty. She could get sick. So, again, I answered, "So-so."

"Well, you must eat first so you can take the medicine on time afterward. Remember, the doctor said we must follow his instructions precisely."

I held the plate with difficulty and began to eat slowly, as slow as a tablespoon every ten minutes, maybe.

That night, before going to sleep, my sister Mayra brought me a cup of milk.

"Evelyn, Mom says to take this milk together with this sleeping pill."

I took the pill around nine at night. With some difficulty, I managed to fall asleep.

When I woke up, I looked at the clock on the wall. It was almost one in the morning. The pill had helped me sleep for only four hours. There was an eternity between one o'clock and dawn.

Upon waking, this massive nervousness washed over me. I felt like my body was swelling. I started feeling pressure from the inside of me, as if my internal organs were pressing to get out. My body was shaking like Jell-O on a plate.

With great effort, I managed to sit up. I did breathing exercises again and again, but I couldn't calm myself down. I realized I needed to divert my attention to something else, or I would lose myself and start screaming in desperation. So, I grabbed the two medicine boxes on my nightstand and took out the medication guide. In each box were two large sheets of paper folded in four. I gave myself the task of reading every line, every sentence, and every single word written in those fact sheets. I read those papers over and over again. I think I must have read them about a dozen times each or so.

It was the third day of treatment. I was getting worse and worse as time passed by. That morning, Mom brought me breakfast again. When she looked at me, her face expressed concern. She held my hand and exclaimed, "Your hands are freezing! You are not feeling well, I can tell."

I asked her to give me some water. I tried to sit up to drink it, but I didn't have the strength. Mom helped me sit up and drink the water.

"How bad are you feeling? Answer me, Evelyn, tell me the truth."

It was impossible for me to hide the gloomy state I was in anymore. I had to answer truthfully.

"I feel dreadful."

"So, I'm telling you, you're no longer going to take these medicines; they are making you worse. Right now, I'm going to call the doctor, and I'll speak with him very seriously. I don't think he knows what he's doing."

While my mother was talking, I went over the doctor's words, "If you promise to follow the treatment all the way, I assure you will be cured."

I wanted to regain my health, and nobody else had made me this promise. I understood it was either this treatment or total hopelessness that could lead me to do something radical. I had no choice but to continue with what I had agreed upon.

In a weak voice, I asked Mom not to call the doctor. I said I believed in him and I was going to continue with the treatment.

"But honey, this is hurting you more."

"Dr. E. assured me this is the treatment I must follow to heal finally. I trust him, Mom. Give me the medicines, please."

"All right, darling. If that's your decision, we must go on. The only thing left for you is to pray for the strength to keep going."

She handed me a rosary she had on the nightstand. Then she left the bedroom quickly.

I took the rosary firmly and began to pray in silence. Thick tears sprouted from my eyes, making the bed sheets wet. Another long night awaited me, and this one promised to be worse than the previous ones.

It was the fourth day of treatment. My muscles felt hard to the touch, and every single cell in my body hurt. It felt as if my body had been wrapped with thick ropes, and they were making them tighter and tighter by the minute. My head felt so heavy I was not even able to lift it. I was gasping for air. My nervous system was on fire, and I felt terrible in my own skin. I wished I could jump out of my body so I wouldn't feel what I was feeling.

Without imagining what was coming, my family was about to witness the first of several shocking scenarios related to the treatment I was receiving.

As in the previous days, Mom came into the room with breakfast. She put it on the table and then leaned over to help me sit up. Suddenly, without even meaning to, I grasped my mom's blouse, and with a heartrending cry, I begged for help.

"Help me, Mom, help me. I can't take it anymore!"

Mom was shocked. Her face showed panic. She held me and looked back to see if there was somebody else who could help her. Right away, she started screaming for help. She went through the list of my sister's names, calling all of them: "Melina, Mayra, Lucy, someone come to help me! Your sister's got worse!"

Everyone ran into the room, visually alarmed by the screams.

"What's wrong, what's wrong, Mom?" they all asked.

"Look at Evelyn; she's got really bad! Help me sit her up."

I was still clinging to my mother's blouse. My cry was more like a moan. It was intense, so profound. I myself was horrified!

Amid her despair, Mom began to give orders. "Rosie, bring fresh water and some handkerchiefs, quickly! Melina, call that doctor right away. Mayra, sit next to her and help me hold her."

Lucy and Rosie put wet handkerchiefs on my forehead and helped me drink some fresh water. Mayra, who was sitting next to me, rubbed my back. Everyone was doing something to help.

Shortly after, I heard someone say, "Mom, Mom, what's wrong?"

Then someone else said, "Let's get her to her bedroom. She needs her blood pressure medicine. Hurry!"

It was total chaos.

Later, Melina returned and told us she had contacted Dr. E. over the phone.

"Evelyn, I talked to the psychiatrist. He told me what had just happened was a reaction to the medicine, and it was normal. We shouldn't be concerned. He prescribed you an anxiolytic. He also warned me not to give it to you frequently because it can cause addiction."

I took the anxiolytic. Minutes later, I fell asleep.

On the fifth day of treatment, the youngest of my nieces came to see me. Dalia wasn't quite four yet; she was my beloved. I used to enjoy playing with her so much, and her witticisms always made me laugh. Mom knew I loved this girl so much, so I guess she thought bringing Dalia over would help lift my spirits.

"Evelyn, you have a visitor I'm sure you are going to like. Come in, Dalia. Sweetie, say hello to your aunt."

"Hello, Aunt Evelyn. I brought my dolls and other toys to play with you."

Mom put Dalia on my bed. She sat next to me and started taking her toys out of her toy purse.

Then Mom said, "Dalia, play with your aunt for a little while, please. Take care of her, okay? She's a little sick." Then, she left.

Dalia began talking to me and playing with her dolls. I just watched the little girl play. The image I saw was like that of an old movie, almost in black and white and in slow motion.

Then, Dalia showed her dolls to me. I didn't feel my voice would sound normal, so I just stared at her and made a huge effort to smile so the little girl wouldn't think I was ignoring her. It was all I could do. I couldn't respond to the girl's attempts to get me to join her game. Good thing it didn't seem to bother her as she continued playing. In her innocence, she couldn't realize in those moments that I was not me; it was just my shell. All the ability to enjoy anything had been removed and erased from my entire being. My brain had no recollection of what joy felt like.

At the beginning of the sixth day, Mom suggested that I get out of bed and go eat breakfast at the dining room table. I was weak and shaky, but I agreed anyway. Two of my sisters held me and helped me stand up and walk.

In the dining room, I sat down and just looked at the milk and the sandwich they had served me. Another challenge in front of me: I had to eat. When I was healthy, I had always loved food. Never in my wildest dreams would I have thought that one day, eating would feel like a punishment to me.

Minutes passed. Mom came back and saw I hadn't even touched the food.

"Eat half the sandwich and drink half a cup of milk at least, honey. I can't give you the medicine on an empty stomach. Try to eat something," she said, almost begging me.

With a lot of difficulty, I took a bite of the bread and a little bit of milk. Mom went back to do some chores. I had no interest in food. I just kept staring at it. My feelings for the food were similar to my feelings toward the table or the chairs in the dining room. Mom came back and, for the second time, saw I still wasn't eating. She held my hands and helped me lift the cup and put it in my mouth. She kept holding my hands until I managed to drink some more of the milk.

Afterward, I asked for help to get back to my room. I lay down on the bed and tried to get some rest, but I didn't feel even the slightest relief. I lay on my side. It was uncomfortable. I lay on my other side. Same thing. I sat up, then I lay down again. I kept moving from one position to another, but none was the correct one. My frustration was so intense that I started to pull my hair as if I wanted to rip it from my scalp. But for better or worse, I had so little strength that I couldn't have succeeded in doing so.

SECOND WEEK

It was the day we were to go see Dr. E. for the second time. We went into the office. Mom was holding me by the arm. She greeted the doctor. He invited us to sit down.

"Good afternoon, Evelyn. Ma'am, how are you doing? We have a lot to talk about, right? Tell me how the first week of treatment developed. Did you follow my instructions closely?"

"Of course, doctor," Mom answered. "I personally made sure Evelyn took her medications three times a day, every day, and at the exact same time."

"Good. You need to continue to do that accurately. This type of medicine works in this way. You must be very disciplined with the schedule."

"That is what we will continue doing, doctor. But I need to tell you that the medicines you prescribed caused serious side effects for my daughter."

"I know, ma'am. One of your daughters called me.

Evelyn, don't forget that before we started the treatment, I warned you it wasn't going to be easy. I asked you if you could promise to be brave, and you said yes. The crisis was the normal reaction of the body to the unknown. But it was also confirmation that the medicine had been delivered. It is temporary; it will pass."

At this moment, it seemed to me that Dr. E. was being insensitive. I even felt resentment toward him for not showing any concern about the horrible side effects I had to endure. I felt like complaining to him about the hell I was going through. But I knew if I tried to say a word, I would burst into tears and may again enter a crisis I wouldn't be able to control. I couldn't do anything but listen.

"Ma'am, have you observed any changes in your daughter? Have you noticed any improvement?"

I thought the doctor shouldn't be asking such a question. Improvement?! It sounded absurd to me.

"I think she is a little bit better," Mom answered.

I felt mad at Mom, too, for saying I was better. I don't think she meant to lie, but what she had just said wasn't true.

Mom continued. "Doctor, I want to thank you for the confidence you have passed down to my daughter. I think it has provided her with the strength she needed to keep going with all of this."

"Thank you, ma'am. After having successfully treated hundreds of patients with major depression, I would say my experience gives me such confidence. Now, Evelyn, what can *you* tell me? "Do you feel better, worse, the same? How do you feel?"

I gave the doctor a serious look. I wanted to show him I was upset. I couldn't say a word because I still had the sensation that I would burst into tears if I tried to talk. Finally, with a lot of effort and in an angry voice, I could say the word "WORSE."

"I knew you were going to say that. I know the first weeks are the most difficult, and I'm sorry about what you are going through, but unfortunately, there's no other way for now.

Always remember your promise. I assure you again that I won't leave you until you are completely healed. Tell me, are you going to continue being brave?"

I was tempted to say no. I was terrified, knowing I would have to repeat that week of horror. "What is the alternative?" I thought. Dr. E. was the only one who had promised to return me to the world of the living.

Finally, I just nodded as a sign that I accepted the challenge once more.

Then, he proceeded to prescribe double doses of the same drugs. The same antidepressants that had caused me so much havoc. I tried not to think about what was coming. Double dose, double torture.

I can't remember which antidepressants I was taking, but it certainly was more than one kind. What I do remember is that around the fifth or sixth week of treatment, the doctor made some changes and added Prozac.

At the beginning of this second week of treatment, I took the first new dose. I started to feel my brain inflate like a car tire when they blew air into it. It grew and grew. My head felt hard, huge, and heavy. The internal pressure increased. It felt as though there was no more room left inside my skull. It seemed like more and more air was being forcibly blown into my cells. Again, the pressure on my chest cut off my ability to breathe freely. No blood was running through my veins, but boiling bubbles, instead. In a rapid way, they were making their way through my arteries with such force that it seemed I was tearing off from the inside out. My bed hurt me. I seemed to be lying over sharp nails instead of a mattress. My pillow felt as hard as a rock. It hurt every time I tried to lay my head down. My whole body was shaking uncontrollably.

There was nothing I could do to help myself. There were no more prayers left, no tears that I hadn't shed already. No resource in this world or the universe could cushion my fall. Everything in its own time, they say. This was my time to suffer, my time to accept, my time to be silent, to just exist, to do anything but to live.

*It was funny before. Why isn't it now?

One afternoon I asked for help to go to the living room where the only television set we had was placed. I thought maybe watching television would get my attention and distract me. My siblings were sitting there watching a comedy show. It was everyone's favorite, *El Chavo del Ocho* (The Boy of House # 8). I sat down and tried to pay attention, too. The show didn't catch my interest at all. At a certain point, everyone started laughing; I couldn't see why. Therefore, I began to observe them. A big smile seemed to have been drawn on each of their faces. Soon after, they weren't only smiling; they were laughing out loud. They were enjoying the show so much that even their bodies expressed it. They threw themselves back and forth on the couch and clapped at the same time. Their laughter became more intense and noisier.

Nonetheless, I couldn't perceive anything funny in what I was seeing. I could hear and understand perfectly what was being said, and I even realized it was a rerun. I had also laughed and enjoyed that same show before. But for some wicked reason, I couldn't feel any excitement this time. To me, everything they were saying or doing in the show was silly, absurd, and pointless. But everybody else found it hilarious.

Realizing that no one else could feel the way I was feeling was chilling. I felt like I was living in another dimension. In a world where I was the only inhabitant. I felt alone in a place without laughter, without colors, without flavors. A world without health, without peace, without family, without friends, without any pleasures. A parallel world created only for me, from where I could just observe others live. I would compare my feelings with Ariel's, the Little Mermaid, "… wish I were part of their world."

A new day arrived the next morning. I wondered what it would bring. My sister Mayra brought my breakfast early in the morning. I asked her to leave it on the nightstand. I promised I would eat it in a little while. Later, she came back and realized I hadn't eaten anything. The milk was now cold, and Mayra had to reheat it. After she brought back the milk, she tried to make sure I drank it, so she helped me sit up and hold the cup of milk. I made an effort to drink most of the milk. As Mayra was helping me lie back down, I felt my stomach churn. I felt like I was going to throw up. I tried to hold it back, but I couldn't. Mayra's clothes got all wet. I could see the expressions of disgust on her face while she was still holding me. Right after, she screamed for help. All my sisters came into the room, very alarmed once more.

Right after, they all started helping. They brought clean clothes and helped me change. My sisters changed all the bedding, too. They also needed to clean and disinfect the floor while Mayra went to shower and change. At home, everyone was being negatively affected by these disturbing scenarios. And I knew it was my fault, even though I wasn't doing it on purpose.

It was past midnight. I hadn't been able to close my eyes. Despite having taken the sleeping pills, I still couldn't get to sleep. Later, I needed to go to the bathroom. I was going to have to go by myself since everyone else was sleeping. I got up as best as I could. I held onto the bed first, then onto the walls. I was about to get to the bathroom when I tripped over something that made me fall. As I fell, I knocked over a chair, and it, in turn, hit other things. In the silence of the night, that fall was thunderous. Everyone woke up at once and came to see what had happened.

"What happened?" everybody asked.

I had woken up everyone. I had disturbed them even while they were sleeping. Knowing I was causing so much distress to the ones I loved made me realize I needed an outlet to express all the guilt and shame I had accumulated in those days. Eventually, I started writing in my journal.

*My Journal – Excerpt 1

"... I cling tooth and nail to the doctor's promise. I need to convince myself that this agony is going to end. But I have a question: will I

be able to resist the time that is remaining? It's been almost two weeks since the start of the treatment, but it seems like an eternity to me. I feel beyond exhausted as if all my energy had been vacuumed off my body and my soul… As soon as I open my eyes in the morning, my fight begins. Every day, I am fighting this nervousness and muscle tension that won't let go of me for a single second…

Today, I've got a sore throat again. What else will come?"

THIRD WEEK

Two long weeks of pure torture had passed. It was time to go see Dr. E. again.

"Go ahead, have a seat. Hello Evelyn. You look much better now."

"I think so too, doctor," intervened my mom. "She is improving. Little by little, she is regaining her physical strength."

I was able to do some talking by now. However, my voice was still kind of shaky. "I feel just as bad. This muscle tension is wearing me out."

"In advanced cases like yours, improvement is not evident, at least for the first weeks. You know, this treatment is a process with steps. You can think of each week as a new step you have just climbed. Unfortunately, so far, there are no shortcuts. I suggest you start writing every day to document how you feel. That way, we can track the changes and advances in your health more closely."

"I just started my journal. I have been writing already."

"Good, I am glad you are willing to write. Starting next week, it would help if you let me read your notes. You can choose what I can read, and if there is something you wouldn't like to show me, that is okay, too."

Mom had something to say, "Doctor, I think you should tell Evelyn to start doing some activities, simple ones, instead of spending hours lying in bed looking at the ceiling. I believe she's doing too much thinking when she is in that position. It is causing her to feel more ill. For example, she's been complaining about having a sore throat, too. Please, tell her she must do her part and stop overthinking."

"Ma'am, you can't ask Evelyn to do her part because she has done everything in her power already. She is actually making an extraordinary effort, believe me!" Dr. E. got serious as he was saying it. "There are occasions in which patients may experience sort of paralysis. This kind of paralysis is a characteristic in the more serious cases of major depression. This is why you see her lying down, looking at the ceiling without moving or doing anything else. It's not because she's choosing not to do anything; it's because, in those moments, she just can't."

The doctor's response to my mom's point of view made me trust him even more than before. I was definitely convinced this man knew exactly how I was feeling.

My mom's eyes went wide open as she listened to the doctor.

"We shouldn't expect her to do things that are not under her control. If you asked someone with a serious spinal cord injury to stand up, what do you think would happen?"

"They would fall."

"Exactly. You should think similarly about your daughter's condition. Now, Evelyn, let me examine your throat."

(I should clarify that the concept of paralysis, in this context, is not to be taken literally. There are moments when we are lying in bed, feeling paralyzed because we don't have the minimum strength necessary to make a single move. Nonetheless, with help from somebody else, we can move and walk. Some people have reported falling on the floor while being home alone and then having to stay there for hours without being able to get up).

The doctor got his tiny flashlight and looked in my mouth.

"I see signs of an infection in your tonsils, Evelyn. Ma'am, you see, she does have her tonsils infected. She hasn't been imagining symptoms."

My mom looked like a child being reprimanded.

"I am going to prescribe antibiotics, too. Evelyn, keep in mind that despite not feeling improvement, it's a fact we are making progress."

(I want to add that strep throat continued coming and going for a few more years. Eventually, I had my tonsils removed).

After all the truths he had told me about my condition, I felt like Dr. E. had the ability to cross the line and jump into the parallel world I was in. I felt like he was accompanying me in this exile.

I began putting more emphasis on documenting this time of sorrow. That little notebook became my personal therapist. It became the only friend to whom I could tell everything about myself. I drew my pain on its sheets. That journal helped me bring out all my frustrations, all my resentments. I asked it questions about this odyssey I was living. In it, I cursed, as well as implored life to have compassion for me. Little did I know that with the help of this friend made of paper, decades later, I was going to be able to tell my story.

*An anxiety crisis

Early one afternoon, my mom, one of my sisters, two of my little nieces, and I were sitting in the living room. My family tried to talk about positive things only, no sad topics or bad news. They needed to shake off that negative energy that had settled in my house over the last few weeks.

There I was, sitting on the sofa. My body felt stiff, but inside me, my nervous system was bubbling. One of the little girls asked my mom, "Grandma, I want to go to the beach. When are you taking me there? It's already summertime."

"Why don't you ask your mom and dad to take you, sweetie?"

"I want to go with you. Let's go to the beach. Please? Please?"

"For now, I can't," Mom replied. "You know, your aunt Evelyn is a little sick. I need to be home to take care of her. Let's wait for her to feel better, and then we all will go to the beach together!"

My other niece came to me and said, "Aunt Evelyn, get better soon so we can go to the beach, pleeease!"

I simply nodded to agree with what the girls were asking for. But things wouldn't stop there. This conversation kept echoing in my head. I kept processing what I had just heard: "When I feel better… when I heal…, will I ever feel as good as they expect? What if I don't improve? What's going to happen to me? What am I going to do?..."

These thoughts rushed at me one after another, assaulting me. The anxiety began to invade me. I felt anguish, fear, and desperation expand rapidly. All the muscles in my body got even more tense, and my breathing turned fast. I was trying to dismiss these horrible thoughts and feelings. I needed to calm down so I wouldn't scare my little nieces. Instead, I started to shake. I tried and tried, but it became more and more difficult to calm myself down.

Mom realized I was entering another anxiety crisis. She stood up and started giving orders.

"Rose, take the girls out quickly."

Unable to hold back anymore, I exploded in tears and groans. Mom held me and began calling for help again. Everybody in the house ran toward the living room. One by one, my siblings started to show, visibly alarmed as they did every time this scenario repeated itself.

My body temperature rose, and I felt hot, like I was sitting beside a bonfire. The tightness in my chest kept increasing, and I was having trouble breathing. Things escalated to the point that I felt like I was suffocating. I tried to get on my feet. I wanted to run anywhere I could find the oxygen I needed, but two of my sisters held me down. I was fighting with all my might to free myself. I wasn't trying to do anything weird; I just needed to feel I could breathe. But how were they to know?

*My Journal – Excerpt 2

"*My entire body feels sore. My legs, the most.*

Is there something I am interested in doing today?

Nothing at all!

Is there any food I crave now?

None. Food isn't exciting anymore. No desire for it.

Why do people believe this life is worth living?

To me, nothing makes sense. We spend most of our time working hard so we can have what we want to eat, and then eat so we can go to work, and the same music is played over and over again. Maybe I should stop trying.

I feel like I'm living in the wrong world. Maybe I really don't belong here, and this is why life doesn't feel like a gift to me but rather a curse. Perhaps somehow, somewhere, somebody miscalculated and sent me into this life by mistake.

I am living in a perpetual state of punishment. Everything is so difficult to do. Getting out of bed is difficult, and moving around is difficult. Showering is an excruciating, energy-demanding task. It feels like I'm carrying an elephant on my back while trying to jump in the shower. And the animal gets even heavier while trying to bend over to wash my feet.

Getting dressed takes forever. Once I manage to put on a single piece of clothing, I fall on the bed, totally exhausted. Then I need to make another effort to put myself together and see if I can regain some energy to continue with the next piece. How much longer will I have to put up with this?"

* Stress-Driven Neurobiological Illness and EATING DISORDERS

About one percent of all American women will develop anorexia, and 1.5 percent will develop bulimia. The National Association of Anorexia Nervosa and Associated Disorders (ANAD) estimates that at least 30 million Americans are living with an eating disorder.

Eating disorders co-occur with depression, and 50 – 70 percent of people suffering from an eating disorder will also experience symptoms of depression. Likewise, individuals with major depressive disorder experience drastic appetite changes. Although they differ in some symptoms, both people with depression and with eating disorders develop an unhealthy relationship with food.

It's not always clear which came first, depression or the eating disorder, mainly because the factors that precipitate both disorders are almost exactly the same. Researchers believe that eating disorders result from a combination of genetics, psychological factors, and societal influences. According to the National Eating Disorder Association (NEDA), "Those with a close relative with an eating disorder are more likely to develop one."

Sometimes, people's depression and anxiety aren't serious enough to prevent them from functioning day by day. When these problems transition into an eating disorder, depression and anxiety also intensify.

Is it possible that all these disorders are simply different expressions of the same problem?

I have watched many videos of girls suffering from anorexia, where they describe their physical symptoms and their emotional nightmares. I realized their havoc aligned perfectly with mine. What they were saying about their debilitating struggles was similar to what I would say about my own. They were describing the way I, myself, used to feel when I was going through a crippling episode of major depression. The difference between them and me is the fact that I wasn't eating because my brain wouldn't crave any food. And these other girls wouldn't eat, possibly because of the overwhelming fear response of their brains to gaining weight.

Some people are judgmental of individuals with eating disorders, thinking they are exercising their free will when they stop eating. We need to open our minds and think that doing something that can cause medical complications, something that is destroying their lives, something that causes them terrible pain and suffering and can even cause death, CAN'T BE FREE WILL!

The NATIONAL INSTITUTE OF MENTAL HEALTH defines eating disorders this way, "Eating disorders are medical illnesses. Genetic and environmental factors can influence eating disorders. It's not a trend or a choice."

Serious eating disorders aren't even about eating too much or not eating at all. They are just symptoms of much deeper underlying biological roots. Some people have reported feeling physically ill after each meal. They said that every time they eat, their anxiety spikes up, and their brains turn noisy, making them feel confused and unable to concentrate. Others have expressed that the fear of gaining weight is profound, uncontrollable, and paralyzing. Others have said they feel they are living an empty life and losing weight is a challenge or more like an obsession that gives them some sense of purpose.

When dealing with someone with anorexia, for example, we are so wrong when we think the solution is to have the person eat. There are cases in which the affected person restarts eating just to please her/his loved ones. Nonetheless, it doesn't mean the ill person has stopped feeling miserable. In a well-documented video, a young woman states that when she was hospitalized due to the seriousness of her anorexia, she obeyed all the instructions given by her physicians. Soon, she reached the target weight. She said she was obedient just so they would discharge her and she could go back home and stop eating again.

You will find the above information in the following YouTube videos:

EATING DISORDERS FROM THE INSIDE OUT

Laura Hill. Ph.D. 2013.

ATHLETE TO ANOREXIA TO ATHLETE

Bex's anorexia recovery. 2021.

Apart from anorexia nervosa and bulimia nervosa, the DSM-5 has listed additional Feeding and Eating Disorders such as binge-eating disorder, avoidant/restrictive food intake, rumination disorder, Pica, and other specified and unspecified feeding or eating disorders.

Anorexia is characterized by severe food restriction. This could be limiting the amount of food or types of food. Not all individuals with anorexia have a distorted body image. There are those who expressed they could see they looked like a skeleton, but still, they kept feeling they shouldn't eat.

Bulimia involves a cycle of binge eating followed by compensatory behaviors such as self-induced vomiting, excessive exercise, or severely restricting food intake. It also includes people's dissatisfaction with their own body image.

Avoidant/Restrictive food intake disorder (ARFID) is diagnosed when a person's avoidance or restriction of food intake is associated with conditions including significant weight loss, nutritional deficiency, or dependence on tube feeding or oral nutritional supplements.

Binge-eating disorder is about consuming unusually large amounts of food and feeling unable to stop eating. You feel such a compulsion that you can't resist the urges. Anxiety and stress may play a role. Carbohydrates can decrease the release of stress hormones, and they can help us release some tension. Therefore, people can get addicted to the soothing sensation that carbohydrates can cause. This would explain why we tend to eat more when we are feeling stressed (Although refined carbohydrates in combination with excess sugar can cause the opposite effect in the long run). Unlike bulimia, people don't compensate for the extra calories.

Pica is an eating disorder that involves eating items that are not typically thought of as food and do not contain significant nutritional value (National Eating Disorders.org). People crave and chew clay, dirt, soil, paper, chalk, eggshells, hair, pet food, and wool. This disorder may be caused by genetic factors, stress, anxiety, and nutritional deficiencies, including calcium and zinc. Also, pregnancy and sickle cell anemia.

Although **severe** eating disorders have certain differences, they are essentially branches of the same tree. They all scream biology.

I would like to say to people with serious eating disorders, "My heart is with you! I feel afflicted every time I see anybody going through such a debilitating battle. I know you are not pretending. I know you are terribly ill, and I know how incomprehensible these diseases of the nervous system can be, especially when they are approached merely as behavioral issues."

FOURTH WEEK

At the doctor's office, Mom said, "Dr. E., I still can't understand why a young woman like Evelyn can have depression. It would be understandable coming from a person with big responsibilities, like me, a mother of ten kids. I have felt depressed from time to time due to the endless challenges of having to work and raise my children at the same time. But Evelyn doesn't have big responsibilities, no main worries. And she always says she is pleased with everything she is doing. I can't make sense of it."

"Ma'am, depression is not only sadness or emotional distress. And that isn't the core issue with your daughter. Her problem is way more complex. She's ill with a real disease that results from abnormal biological changes. They can affect the normal functions of the brain."

"I had never heard this before. And why is this thing happening to her?"

"As you told me the other day, a sibling had the disease before her; this means she has inherited this same disease."

"I never thought people could inherit depression."

"MDD is a heritable disease," emphasized the doctor. "People get the genes from their parents."

"Really? They must have come from her father's side," said Mom defensively.

Dr. E. turned to me and started asking questions. "Tell me, Evelyn, have you been writing in your journal regularly?"

"Yes, doctor. That's mostly what I have been doing every day, most of the day. It is almost the only thing I feel worth doing."

"That's not bad. The more details you use to describe how you feel, the better. That way, I can track your progress."

"Doctor, is this nightmare ever going to end?" I asked. "This muscle tension, the nervousness, the fact that I can't calm myself down, it's just unbearable!"

"Little by little, Evelyn. Remember that when you first came to see me, you were very ill. Your case was very serious. Let me explain. Before starting treatment, your brain was like a person severely malnourished; the medicines you are taking now represent vitamins for the brain. Now, the more advanced the malnutrition, the longer it takes to reverse it. That's why it's going to take a little longer for you to get back to normal."

"At least I would like to be able to sleep through the night. Will you increase the dose of sleeping pills, please?"

"We will see. At this point, because you are getting more mobile, you should start going for walks. Go to a park, observe the landscape and the people, and breathe the fresh air. This way, you can divert your attention to the external world and think less about your internal one."

I just nodded, but going for walks still felt like a big task for me. Just thinking about the effort it would take made me feel tired already.

*My Journal – Excerpt 3

"Why should I make such an effort to advance today if tomorrow I will have to start from scratch again? I don't live life; I suffer life. My nightmare doesn't start when I fall asleep but rather when I wake up. Immediately, anxiety and anguish seize me. It's so

frightening to have to constantly deal with these executioners who keep getting bigger and stronger while I get smaller and weaker...

Since I was a child, I have heard people label anyone who suffered from a mental illness 'crazy'... They also said the 'crazy' don't know what they do or what they say. They are disconnected from reality. So, I guess people with mental illness don't suffer because they aren't aware of what is happening to them. This would mean I'm not mentally ill because I am very aware of what is happening to me. If it's true that the 'crazy' don't suffer, I wish I were crazy!"

*What does teen depression look like?

The US CDC reports that 15.1 percent of adolescents aged 12-17 years had a major depressive disorder between 2018 and 2019. And 36.7 percent had persistent feelings of sadness and hopelessness.

At some point during my meetings with Dr. E., I told him about the struggles I went through in my teens because of the disease.

"I was thirteen years old. I was about to start junior high in a girls-only school, as it had always been for me. However, major changes were happening. I was going to a new school, I would meet new friends, and I would encounter a new teaching system. In primary school, we had one single teacher for all the courses; now, we would have multiple teachers, one for each school subject.

It was the first day of class. Upon arrival, we had to stay outside the classrooms, at the big recess patio, for quite some time. We were waiting for the school principal to deliver a speech welcoming the new school year. Members of the administrative department also talked and gave us insight into the school dynamics. Finally, they assigned a classroom number to each group of students. Some of our teachers came over to introduce themselves. I got to see my new classmates, and I also saw some familiar faces. We must have had around thirty girls in that classroom. The setting was crowded, too. There were several tables and many chairs. Up front, there was a big green chalkboard and a teacher's desk. The feature that stood out was the not-very-pleasant-looking corrugated metal ceiling. On the second day, a new teacher arrived. She introduced herself and told us that she was the History and Geography teacher. Then she called the roll. After that, the teacher suggested rearranging the classroom setting. She told us to move the tables and chairs to create more space to walk through.

There were four chairs for each table. Nonetheless, there were five chairs at my table; we were five girls instead of four. Pointing to my table, the teacher said the groups should be four. Therefore, there was an extra girl in my group. Then she grabbed a dirty, individual desk chair that was abandoned in a corner. The teacher said, 'One of you is going to have to move to this chair.' We looked at one another, thinking who was going to be the one. Apparently, the other four girls in the group already knew each other. I was new. In pairs, they held hands while saying to each other, 'Not you, not you, stay.'

Seeing that, the teacher pointed to me and ordered me to leave the group and go sit on that individual desk chair, now placed back in the corner. So now I was alone, everybody was working in groups but me. I was isolated.

That moment was very shocking to me. I felt rejected. I felt unwanted and even humiliated. I started to feel physically ill. My body temperature would rise and rise, my heartbeat was progressively accelerating, and I started feeling a strong pressure on my chest. I felt I was going to burst into tears at any moment. But I had to prevent that from happening because I knew it would be very embarrassing if my classmates saw me cry over something apparently meaningless.

During that class, all my attention was committed to preventing a single tear from falling from my eyes. I resisted with all my will. Finally, the class ended. I could hardly remember what it was about.

From that day on, I continued experiencing unwanted, horrible emotions. From that corner, I could see all the other girls interacting with each other while I was by myself, feeling discriminated against, like someone with a communicable illness in quarantine. Trying to avoid revealing my emotions got harder and harder. It demanded a lot of willpower from me. Attending school had turned into an ongoing struggle.

The moment came when I could no longer continue concealing my despair. So, all that repressed anguish caught up with me very badly. Tears began to flow from my eyes and then rolled down my cheeks. I immediately started to dry them with my hands and did my best to stop them, but more sprouted.

When the teacher asked me why I was crying, I came up with the excuse that I had a headache. She recommended that I rest my head on the desk and wait to see if it went away.

That situation kept repeating as days passed. I no longer had the slightest control over my crying. Later, the crying turned into sobs. The school called Mom in and informed her about what was going on with me.

For some reason, I still don't understand; I couldn't explain to my mom what had triggered my distress. I guess it didn't sound like a valid argument if it didn't make any sense to me, or maybe I felt nobody else would consider it bad enough to result in such a loss of control.

I ended up telling Mom I was missing my old friends, my old school, and my teachers. She said that was normal. I shouldn't worry, and it would soon pass.

The situation didn't improve, though. Things got so bad that now I started feeling ill even before I was in school. As the time to go to school approached, I was assaulted by the anxiety of knowing a horrible school day was awaiting me. Every day, while I was walking to school, I saw all the other boys and girls walking by me, interacting with one another. They looked happy and comfortable with what was going on around them. I, however, felt like an observer. I was aware I wasn't having the same experiences.

Dozens of students would walk to school every day at the same time. The noise they made bothered me, and even the smell of food on the streets was unpleasant. Every day, I wondered why I couldn't feel relaxed and able to share their excitement.

One day, as I was putting on my school uniform, Mom saw me crying. She asked me, 'Why are you crying now? It can't be because you are missing your friends. You're not even at school yet.'

'I don't know. I just feel this pressure on my chest and the urge to cry.'

My mom brought me to see the doctor at the community medical center.

The doctor asked me why I was crying, and I responded the same, 'I don't know why.'

'Nobody cries because of nothing,' he exclaimed.

I wanted to express what was happening to me, but I couldn't find the way. Everything seemed absurd to me. What would I say that made sense?

This doctor assumed I was crying because maybe I had a special little boyfriend. And maybe we had had a fight.

Mom didn't buy such an assumption at all.

Eventually, she took me to see a psychiatrist. She herself had seen one in the past.

The doctor asked me simple questions and gave me small tasks like telling him what day it was, repeating a sequence of numbers like 8-3-9-1-6-4-2, and repeating a series of numbers backward. I didn't have any trouble with my answers.

The doctor concluded it was just teen depression. He prescribed some medication and asked us to come back the following week.

Mom decided I shouldn't take medicine. She believed it was dangerous for me to take psychiatric medicine at such a young age. Therefore, we didn't go back to see the psychiatrist again.

Then, Mom talked to the Dean of Students. Mom told her the doctor had said my problem was only emotional, and I just needed a little time to adapt to the new changes.

All the teachers were informed of my situation, so they would let me cry freely. They would simply ignore me.

I had to continue attending school under such conditions with no other option. Mom had already decided I wasn't going to see the psychiatrist again, nor was I going to take any medication. Dropping out of school didn't even cross my mind.

My struggles continued for quite a while. I don't recall when the crying and everything else that made me feel so miserable finally stopped."

FIFTH WEEK

Every week, when it was time to see my psychiatrist again, I had the expectation that this time, the doctor would finally give me something that would make a difference and have a huge impact on my recovery. I was longing for what I really needed: some relief, a pause in this fight.

Dr. E. inquired about the past week, the medications, how I felt, and all the usual follow-up questions.

Mom needed to ask the doctor something. "When my other daughter got sick, I can't say her case was simple, but it certainly wasn't as bad as Evelyn's. Why is Evelyn's depression much more serious?"

"Well," said the doctor, "Not all cases are identical. Actually, most cases have something unique. Several factors play a role and influence the seriousness of the disease. There may have been additional elements that contributed to the development of a more complex version. If we investigate, I'm pretty sure we can find interesting details."

Dr. E. was right. We were about to unveil some things we had never thought about before.

"What else could it be?" asked Mom.

"What about problems during the pregnancy with Evelyn? Did you have any complications? Is there anything important you can remember?"

"No, my pregnancy was normal, no complications. Nonetheless, I remember an anecdote I can tell you about. It was funny rather than serious, I would say. When Evelyn was born, the doctor told me he thought she was premature. With a big smile on my face, I told him, 'Doctor, I know I have been pregnant for nine months; she can't be premature.' The thing is that Evelyn was born very small. She was so tiny that she fit in a size -13 men's shoebox. Her mouth was so narrow that it was difficult for me to feed her. I even had a hard time finding a pacifier small enough for her."

"Wow," said the doctor, showing concern. "Ma'am, did you know that being born that small and underweight is a sign something may have gone wrong during the pregnancy?"

That was jaw-dropping for Mom. "I never knew it was a problem."

"If she was born as small as you are describing, there must have been some issues that prevented her normal development."

The doctor continued, "And what can you tell me about your emotional state during the pregnancy? Were you at ease and relaxed most of the time? Or were you worried and anxious with a lot of problems?"

Mom thought for a moment and then said, "Well, at the time, my older sister was also pregnant. Thus, we were both pleased and enjoying the special moments we were sharing. We were building tons of good memories. Everything was going well.

When I was five months pregnant with Evelyn, the time came for my sister to deliver her baby. At the time more than twenty years ago, many women gave birth at home, cared for by a midwife. They weren't accredited; they were just women with experience helping other women. It was the case with my sister.

There were complications during the delivery. My sister was rushed to the hospital because she was bleeding heavily. By the time she got to the hospital, she had lost much blood. The doctors were doing their best to save her. However, the unimaginable happened. My sister passed away, and her baby didn't survive either. It was a horrific tragedy that shook the whole community in those days.

I got traumatized, mainly when I saw my sister in the coffin and her beautiful baby boy lying by her side. At that point, the whole room turned dark to me. I lost myself. I have no recollection of what happened to me right after that.

The remaining four months of my pregnancy were also difficult to go through."

I added something I had always known, "Her name was Evelyn. Mom named me after her."

Dr. E. looked impressed. He just kept nodding and gave Mom a look that said, "You see, we got the answer to your question."

In this fifth week of treatment, something unusual happened. Mom told me she had received a call from Dante, my ex-boyfriend. He had called to inquire about my health. Dante knew about my situation because during the time we were going out before I got really sick, I never lied to him. I used to tell him how I was feeling, and he witnessed the progression of my disease. As my health continued deteriorating, I decided to end our relationship.

Dante told Mom he was thinking about coming over to see me and inviting me to the movies. He said he believed it would be beneficial for me to go out and get some distraction.

My mom thought it was a good idea, too. Hence, she kept encouraging me to accept the invitation by saying, "Evelyn, I think by now your physical strength is good enough for you to start going places. You have been able to take back some personal responsibilities, including dispensing your own medication. I do not need to worry about it anymore, and you are succeeding in following the doctor's guidelines closely. I think you should accept the invitation."

All those weeks, I hadn't left home except to go see the doctor. I didn't feel like going anywhere, nor did I want anybody to see me. I told Mom I wasn't going to the movies or any other place.

In the days that followed, Mom kept telling me Dante seemed to be a good guy, and he was just trying to help. She pointed out that because he knew about my health issues, I could feel comfortable going out with him, knowing he wouldn't be judgmental. She insisted I should go get some distraction.

The day arrived. Just thinking about everything I had to do to get ready was overwhelming. I needed to take a shower, wash my hair, get dressed, comb my hair, and put on some makeup so I wouldn't look so bad. I felt there were a hundred steps to follow before I was ready.

Completing any task, even simple ones, required so much effort from me. After completing a task, I needed to rest before I could start a new one. It was taking me a lot of time. It felt like a case of common laziness multiplied by a million.

Dante came to pick me up at around three. Although I had started hours before, I still wasn't ready yet.

*A chilling experience at the movies:

We left home and took a taxi. We arrived at the movie theater. Dante offered to buy me popcorn and soda, but I declined.

I wasn't going to watch a drama or anything unpleasant, so we picked a comedy titled My Girlfriend is an Alien.

The theater was packed. Dante sat to my left and told me the plot, like a spoken preview. The movie started. Soon after, people were laughing. It didn't seem funny to me, but at least I was able to focus and follow the plot. Everything was going smoothly until...

My eyelids grew heavy, and my eyes closed without me trying. I opened them quickly. I was startled by this weird thing that had just happened to me. I kept watching the movie. A little while later, it happened again. My eyelids closed on their own. I started feeling my heart rate accelerate, and my breathing got fast. Immediately, I opened my eyes and intended to keep them that way. For the third time, I felt my eyes closing against my will. I threw my head back on the seat to help prevent this from happening. I tried and tried hard to keep them open. Eventually, my eyes closed completely, and I lost consciousness.

Later, I woke up lying on a couch in the anteroom. I could hear Dante talking to another gentleman who was asking him, "Do you know if she suffers from a condition that causes fainting?"

"I don't think so. She would have told me," Dante replied.

That gentleman, who I later learned was a physician who happened to be in the audience, went on saying, "It seems she's coming to her senses. She's waking up!"

I opened my eyes. My vision was blurry. However, I could see there were many people around us. I could hear a lot of noise, with everyone wanting to know what was happening. I tried to sit up. Dante helped me. At that moment, the doctor told him, "You can take her with you now. Go see her doctor."

"Thank you very much for everything, doctor," said Dante.

"You're welcome." Then, he moved on.

Little by little, the curious people began to withdraw. They were going back to the theater.

The movie was starting over. I sat for a minute, trying to understand what had happened to me.

Then, I saw a young girl approaching, maybe twelve or thirteen years old. She extended her hand and delivered something, saying, "Here you are; I found it on the floor."

It was one of my shoes.

Minutes later, we headed to the doctor's office. Dr. E. was genuinely nice to see me without an appointment.

"Evelyn, the nurse took your blood pressure; it is normal. Your pulse is normal, too. You don't have a fever, and nothing hurts, right? Everything seems to be fine. Did you drink alcohol by any chance?"

"No, doctor, I assure you, not a single drop. I have never been a fan of alcohol, anyway."

Dante chimed in, "Excuse me, doctor, the situation was very scary to me. I thought she was dying. Could it be that some medicine is having a negative effect on her? Is fainting one possible side effect?"

Dr. E. responded, "Taking any medication carries some risk, especially those targeting the brain. It's the most influential organ in our body. Antidepressants are serious medications. They should be used only when it is strictly necessary. As a doctor, I must weigh the benefits and the risks for the patient. In Evelyn's case, the scale tips decisively toward the benefits."

Dr. E. continued, "Evelyn, do you have your medicine with you now?"

"No, doctor, I was going to take the last dose of the day when I returned home."

"I think I explained to your family they had to be very disciplined with the hours you take your medicine. Who is in charge of dispensing your medication at home?"

"I have been doing it myself."

"What time did you take the afternoon dose?"

I tried to recall at that moment, but I couldn't find anything in my memory.

"It means you didn't take the afternoon dose, right?"

I just nodded.

"And what time did you take the medicine in the morning?"

For the second time, I remained silent, trying to remember that moment, but I couldn't. It was evident I hadn't taken the medicine in the morning either. I felt so embarrassed. Apparently, having to get ready to go out with Dante had overwhelmed me in such a way that it didn't leave room in my mind to remember to take my meds.

Dr. E. said, "Your family will have to take over again and administer the medication on time."

My Journal – Excerpt 4

"I feel like I have been running a marathon for years without stopping. Although I want to abandon this race, I simply can't. My body doesn't obey me. I could be a character in some mythology, 'The woman who couldn't ever feel rested.'

My nervous system is on edge. It feels like boiling water is running through my veins. My muscles feel tight to the point where it hurts. I can't feel at ease for a second. This is such a torment!

This hole I am in now is deep and wide. It's dark; it's cold and, above all, slippery. I find myself trying to climb up all the time, but my efforts are useless. Even when I manage to climb half the way, I always slip down and end up at the bottom. I don't feel I can try again."

SIXTH WEEK

At the beginning of the sixth week, I was more mobile. For the first time since I had started treatment with Dr. E., I was able to take a taxi all by myself and go to his office without my mother. Dr. E. was very pleased to hear about my progress.

"I'm so glad to see you can already mobilize by yourself. Have you been getting out of your house frequently?"

"Yes, doctor. Being able to move on my own helps. For example, when I feel like my levels of anxiety are about to overflow, I leave home and walk and walk without caring where I am going. It helps me breathe and release some tension."

"That's an effective way of coping with anxiety."

"One day, while I was walking aimlessly, it occurred to me I could ride the bus. I rode the bus all the way to the terminal. Then I took the next bus back. I could distract myself for a few hours at least."

"I'm very proud of you as my patient. It's a good idea to look for new methods of self-help. You keep doing what works for you and discard whatever doesn't."

"Doctor, before I forget, I need to ask you something.

*Is it true antidepressants cause addiction?"

"Where have you heard that?"

"On television. Someone said antidepressants are highly addictive. And, whoever decides to take them should know it is going to be very difficult for them to get off this type of medicine."

The doctor said, "It is unbelievable how people who know nothing about this topic dare to give their opinions. Antidepressants aren't addictive at all. You'll see how easy it is to get off the antidepressants once you don't need them anymore. Of course, nobody should stop taking antidepressants cold turkey. That isn't the way to do it. But it has nothing to do with addiction. Don't listen to the nonsense some people say."

"Okay, doctor. I definitely believe you; you are the expert."

I had been looking for more details about my disease and had read some articles and heard more things about treatments for MDD. I took the opportunity to ask Dr. E. about this all.

"Doctor, I need to ask you one more question."

"Ok. What else have you heard?" inquired Dr. E. in a subtle tone of annoyance.

"Well, I have also read that antidepressants aren't the best treatment for depression because after stopping them, the depression always comes back."

"Really?" exclaimed Dr. E. in disbelief.

"You know what? I didn't know there was such a level of baseless information going around. I wonder who could've come up with so much inaccuracy and why?"

"I'm going to believe whatever you tell me. I just need to hear the truth from you."

"I have already told you I won't leave you until you get cured. This treatment with antidepressants will result in a cure for your

MDD. Now, will your MDD come back after a few years? Let's consider someone who is given chemotherapy for cancer. The treatment was a success, and the patient is now cancer-free. Will the cancer come back in the future? Who can know that?

A recurrent MDD would depend on many things. On how well you've been taking care of yourself. But the biological changes aren't always under the patient's control."

"I see. Well, I never took medicine when I got depression in my childhood, nor did I receive treatment during my teen years. This is the third and worst depression episode I have had. Therefore, untreated MDD can also come back."

"Exactly. I'm glad you understand it."

"Doctor, I am committed to completing the treatment so I can feel healthy. I'll try not to worry about what may happen in the future.

*But what if I relapse?"

"You don't need to worry about it. Nonetheless, after recovering, you'll need to learn techniques to help you prevent relapse."

"One more thing, doctor, this trembling of my hands doesn't go away. Will they ever stay still?"

"It will eventually go away. You shouldn't worry about it."

"Also, I keep wishing I could feel renewed when I wake up in the morning, but it's not happening."

"The worst is over; keep that in mind."

I felt hopeful. However, I still wasn't feeling the way I needed to.

*My Journal – Excerpt 5

"I have been going for walks as my psychiatrist suggested. It demands such a big effort to get dressed, to comb my hair, to tie up my sneakers... There are dozens of steps I must follow just to get ready to go out. Nonetheless, once I am outside, I don't feel like coming back home. I am scared by the deeply strange feelings that take over my body every time I walk through the threshold of the door to enter my home .... "

"... Life hurts. If only someone could get inside of me and take control so I could rest ... My constant struggle to flee from my oppressors is so futile; they always catch up with me. How does it feel to be normal? Does anybody ever sleep through the night? Is it possible to wake up feeling rested? Will I ever feel relaxed? I don't remember how it feels to be happy. Maybe all those feelings don't exist, and people just pretend.... "

*Stress-Driven Neurobiological Illness and SUICIDE

I am going to present some of the misbeliefs surrounding SDNBI and suicide:

a.- Patients have suicidal thoughts or ideation.

When it comes to SDNBI, we don't wake up in the morning thinking, "I believe I'm going to kill myself today." There's no such thing! People with unipolar depression are not psychotic. We don't hear voices telling us to end our lives. We don't see things that don't exist or do things without knowing what we're doing. When people with this disease express that they want to die, what they really mean is, "This is too much; this is unbearable. I can't take it anymore." As it is very difficult to find in our vocabulary the appropriate words that can best describe how intense and sickening our symptoms are, we just repeat what we hear from other people when they feel troubled, "I want to die."

I would like to tell the family and close friends of people who died by suicide (due to a serious case of SDNBI) that their loved ones didn't

Kill themselves; the illness did. They died of this disease. You will better understand what I mean as you keep reading.

b.- Patients of this kind lose their will to live.

We certainly don't want to die. We are dying to live, but we simply can't in such conditions. Most people just want to stop their torment.

But when they feel all their efforts are futile and not even the love of their families manages to take away their despair, then what is the alternative?

Sometimes, when the family and close friends of a person with a severe case of the disease suspect this person might be considering suicide, they concentrate on preventing the person from hurting themselves, which is good. However, staying vigilant just to prevent suicide is peace of mind for the family and friends. But it doesn't make things less difficult for the person in distress.

The very first step, and the most crucial one, is finding out what we are really fighting against. A loving and nonjudgmental conversation is a good start to begin searching for the root causes of the problem. Is it an emotional/psychological issue? Is it environmental? Is the person troubled by a difficulty that needs solving? Or is it a medical problem that needs medical treatment?

Patients with this illness of the nervous system don't simply have suicidal thoughts, but rather, **suicidal** physical and emotional **suffering**.

The kind of suffering that keeps pushing us to the edge every day, every hour, every minute, every second, every fraction of a second, so much so that some get to the breaking point and realize they just can't go on. They don't have any trace of energy left to continue the fight, so they make the **conscious decision** to end their torturous internal reality. Although conscious, this decision is not a choice.

"…I claim that any man who commits suicide of necessity suffers more than any who continues to live. I don't want to die. I cannot make any outsiders realize by anything I can write how I have tried to avoid this step…."

WALLACE E. BAKER

Diary of a Suicide

I watched the story of a mother and her teenage son. The mother started by saying her son had always been a well-behaved and loving boy. However, he had shown signs of serious anxiety since he was a child. The mother stated that when her son reached his teens, things got so bad that even ordering a pizza over the phone would make him nervous to the point where he would rather go hungry than pick up the phone and talk to a stranger to order his food.

Being an introvert, he became an easy target for bullies at school. When his parents learned about it, they immediately took charge of the situation and supported him in every way possible. He went to a different school and started psychotherapy. Things seemed to improve.

A few years later, the mother found out he was using illegal drugs. Because of that, she decided to send him to rehab. Some time afterward, things seemed to improve again. But not for long. This young man relapsed. His parents had to send him to rehab for a second time. Upon leaving rehab, he continued with psychotherapy for quite a while.

Time passed, and things went downhill. Psychotherapy was definitely not working for him. He must have been experiencing such a deep level of anguish that he confessed to his mother he was suicidal. The mother hugged him and begged him not to do it because he was going to hurt her too much. She also told him she was no longer going to have peace of mind, thinking she would get a phone call at any moment telling her he had taken his life. "Don't do it to me," she insisted.

Because of his mother's pleas, this boy, who was a young adult now, decided he wasn't going to take his life at the moment. However, he said he couldn't guarantee he wouldn't ever do it. He showed how considerate he was when he promised his mom he would let her know if he ever decided to act. That way, she wouldn't have to worry about it happening at any moment without her knowing first.

The mother stated that when she told his therapist about what happened, this person said to her, "If he told you he's going to kill himself, it means he won't do it." Unfortunately, the mom believed it.

A year later, this young fellow came to his mom and said, "The day has come, Mom." He was doing as he had promised. Again, as much as she could, the mother begged him not to do it. Right after, she called up other family members and told them about the situation. They all came over and talked to him for a while. When they considered they had managed to calm him down and they were convinced the boy wasn't showing any signs of being suicidal anymore, all these people finally left.

The next thing he said to his mother clearly showed the real underlying reason for his decision. He didn't say, "Because I'm a loser, or I'm not worthy, or nobody loves me." None of that. Strongly, he said, "Mom, I AM TIRED!" As we have learned, what this guy really meant was, "I don't have a trace of energy left; I can't take it anymore."

Later that day, he jumped off his tall building.

"External misery has relatively little to do with suicide. The real motives belong to the internal world, ...

Thus, suicide becomes a natural reaction to an unnatural condition."

ALFRED ALVAREZ

The Savage God

Watch the above story in this YouTube video:

EL SUICIDIO DE MI HIJO SE PUDO HABER EVITADO

(My son's suicide could have been prevented).

Mas Allá del Rosa. Jessica Fernandez. Feel Better, Live Better podcast. Nov 7/2018.

I just can't imagine how much turmoil this young man had to put up with all those years without getting the help he really needed. The fact that it never occurred to the parents that their son could have a medical problem is alarming. His mother always talked about therapy and rehab, but she never mentioned seeing a physician to look for biological causes. Especially because he had shown serious anxiety issues since he was a child. Unfortunately, nobody in the family ever thought about a brain image or a functional MRI. It seems they never saw his challenges as a physical disease.

This is the price young people pay for the absence of relevant, up-to-date information and for efforts not being made in the community to educate people about SDNBI. People need to get it truly clear that SDNBI is a potentially lethal medical condition, and overlooking its seriousness is costing too many lives.

I should tell the people who are seriously ill with SDNBI, "If you feel you have reached your breaking point, ask your psychiatrist to help you sleep for an extended period of time. At this point, only sleep can effectively help someone who can't carry on anymore. Stay asleep during the period of time it will take for the medication to take full effect on you. It's better to sleep for a while than to end your life. When the medicine finally shows its full potential, I promise you will feel like you have been born again."

SEVENTH WEEK

According to what the doctor told me at the beginning, the treatment would take between four and six weeks to show its full benefit, but it was still not happening for me. Dr. E. attributed it to the severity of my case. He kept telling me I should be more patient.

I realized I needed to do something more substantial to help myself get through my days, some activities that would help me cope with the body tension, the nervousness, and the anguish stuck in my chest that would overwhelm me so frequently. When I gave this some thought, I got an idea.

In those days, my family had a small food concession business on the premises of a company close to my home. It occurred to me that I could help them with the business's tasks. I decided to ask Mom to let me come with them and help with something.

My mom was hesitant because she wasn't sure if this was going to be beneficial for me. She told me maybe it would be better for me to stay home and rest.

"Rest?!" I exclaimed. "But that's precisely what I can't succeed in doing. I've been making all kinds of efforts to feel rested, and I've not been able to do it. It feels like a curse to me. I need to do something different!"

I was determined, so I kept insisting. Reluctantly, Mom finally agreed to let me come with them.

It was my first day in this new attempt at my survival. I was supposed to get up at five-thirty in the morning. It wasn't going to be easy for me to get up so early, but then I thought it would be the same at five in the evening. Besides, anything was preferable to staying home, feeling like I was drowning all the time.

Once in the place, they assigned me the task of organizing all the glasses and cutlery used to serve the food. I helped my sisters with everything they asked of me. I didn't need to know the daily dynamics; I just needed to follow orders.

Workers came to collect their food, most of them at the same time. There were a lot of employees. It was a fast-paced service, so the servers needed to move fast. The hubbub was increasing. Most of the workers talked and conversed while they waited in line for their food. The tumult was unpleasant to me, but there was no space left to think about anything other than collaborating in every way possible to ensure workers were taken care of efficiently and promptly.

Before finishing for the day, we picked up the dirty pots, cleaned the dining room, and got ready to go back home. We were done around ten. I left the place totally convinced this new occupation would be of great benefit to me.

In my mind, I went through all the good reasons to continue with this occupation:

1. In that place, nobody knew me. Therefore, they couldn't notice any changes in my behavior.

2. I didn't have to make a huge effort to make things look normal with me. I didn't even need to talk.

3. That trembling in my hands went unnoticed simply because all those workers were only focused on getting their food served quickly so they could get back to work.

4.-It was an informal job for me, very different from an office environment or classroom. I could wear a jogging suit and a pair of sneakers, place a headband on my head, no makeup, no need to do my nails or wear jewelry. I was saving the energy I didn't have.

* Why doesn't everybody get ill with SDNBI?

Many times, I have seen people giving talks about this matter. They talked about the individuals who didn't develop depression after trauma as good examples of how we should tackle our misfortunes. They suggested these people succeeded in managing their emotions because, in a way, they were smarter.

And they had figured out how to shake off the burdens of life itself because they were optimists.

After hearing that, I couldn't help feeling they were judging me for having major depression. They were basically saying, "I am weak, I'm not intelligent, and I'm a pessimist who can't see the silver lining, so I'm responsible for my own suffering." The rhetoric that it's possible for all of us to cure ourselves of any disease just by thinking positively is a lie. And many times, it can even be counterproductive. When people don't obtain the expected results, they get demoralized and may fall into a much deeper hole that can lead to a tragic outcome. As a matter of fact, once I read an author who suggested that treating someone who is seriously ill with SDNBI solely with talk therapy should be considered malpractice. I can't help but agree with it.

The mind-over-the-body ideology ignores the fact that optimism alone isn't quite enough to stop the progression of a disease once it has turned so malignant. Placing responsibility or blame on the shoulders of someone who's already struggling to survive is insensitive and even mean.

Suggested YouTube video:

LOSING OUR DAUGHTER TO SUICIDE. Kristen and Jeff Durand.

Grateful Living. 2022.

In this video, these parents talk about their daughter's serious struggle with depression.

They say she was taking talk therapy, but she hated it because she felt it wasn't helping her.

The outcome talks for itself.

Main risk factors

At present, we know the hardware and software sides of the brain have an enormous capacity to influence each other. This means experience can change brain activity. So, if someone born with the deviant gene or genes that put them at a higher risk for this disorder is lucky enough to grow up in an ideal household with love, security, protection, and minimal life difficulties, they will experience positive emotions most of the time as a result. The ongoing positive experiences build up and reinforce brain cell connections of positivity, which makes the nervous system stronger, more resilient, and better equipped to confront stressful situations successfully.

Since positive life experiences produce positive emotions, which then build up positive neural connections, these people can aim for a balanced and peaceful emotional world. A peaceful lifestyle helps prevent problematic genes from expressing themselves and allows optimal genes to turn on. For this reason, the odds that these individuals will develop the illness are limited. (Nonetheless, the genetic load also plays a central role. Individuals born to two parents with SDNBI have a double chance of developing the disease. This could be the case with people who, despite having high standards of living, end up developing the disease anyway).

On the other hand, people who grow up in terrible living conditions, those who have gone through big trauma and whose lives are far from being optimal but who, at the same time, are lucky for not having inherited the dubious genes, can't possibly turn on such genes because they simply don't have them. These people are calm by nature; they don't even need to make much effort not to worry about the negative aspects of their lives. However, it doesn't necessarily mean they have a stronger personality. Being strong means you dare to do things that demand courage.

We may think everything is positive with this type of temperament, but some aspects are not so cool. I have known some laid-back people and noticed they aren't always willing or even interested in conquering challenges that life may bring to them. In addition, some people of this character type may display low levels of sympathy toward the weak and needy. Some may even be inconsiderate (sometimes without intending to). Thus, people with these characteristics are very unlikely to develop a disease of this kind despite the seriousness of their negative experiences.

Also, they always say our genes are not our destiny. However, studies show that some conditions, like Huntington's disease, are 100 percent influenced by genetics. If you inherit the disease gene(s), there's a 100 percent chance you'll develop the disease at a certain point in your life. You may be able to slow down the progression with lifestyle changes and taking medication, but there's nothing you can do to stop it.

Huntington's disease causes the progressive degeneration of the nerve cells in the brain. As the disease advances, it can lead to loss of intellectual abilities, uncontrolled movements, and emotional disturbances. The most common psychiatric disorder associated with the disease is depression. Antidepressants and antianxiety medications may be prescribed to treat these symptoms and prevent suicide, which is common among those with Huntington's disease.

In most cases, it's the interaction of multiple determinants that is more likely to be our destiny. For example, severe early stress can result in drastic alterations in neuroendocrine and behavioral responses, which can cause structural changes in the cerebral cortex. In addition, personality traits are strongly influenced by inheritance. Our deviant genes make us more sensitive to stress and, consequently, more vulnerable. And if we added current harsh life conditions, BINGO! We've got the FORMULA that causes SDNBI (MDD). Genetics loads the gun, and trauma pulls the trigger.

*A Study on the Genetics of SDNBI

They usually say that there's no such thing as depression gene(s). Nonetheless, we don't need to be experts on genetics to infer the opposite. We just need to follow the empirical evidence. Usually, people who develop the disease have, or had, other members of the family with the same illness or other related diseases.

When we refer to the disease as "running in the family," we are stating that such disease is in the family members' DNA.

Therefore, it's a physical illness that has been passed on from the parents to their offspring.

Let's take the example of Ernest Hemingway. After suffering from MDD for many years, he eventually took his life. But he wasn't the only one. Not two, not three, not four, but seven of his family members, including his father and two of his siblings, died by suicide.

We could speculate that maybe they had been sharing an unhealthy environment that made them all sick. This theory would be hard to believe, though. And it wouldn't explain why his granddaughter, the supermodel Margaux Hemingway, who obviously didn't share the same environment, also took her life much later.

A study conducted by Roy Perlis, M.D., M.SC. (Medical doctor and Master of Science), of Harvard/Massachusetts General Hospital found 17 genetic variations linked to depression at 15 genome locations.

Prior to this study in 2016, conventional genome-wide approaches had failed to reliably identify chromosomal sites associated with the illness in populations with European roots. In addition to hinting at a link between depression and brain gene expression during development, there was also evidence of overlap between the genetic basis of depression and other mental illnesses.

"We hope these findings help people understand that depression is a **brain disease** with its own biology," said Perlis. "Now comes the hard work of using these new insights to try to develop better treatments."

EIGHTH WEEK

Dr. E. was very pleased with my decision to try something new. He also thought this new activity would be beneficial for me.

"I'm very happy to hear you have decided to try this new activity. This sounds very promising, Evelyn."

"I think so, too, doctor. I felt I needed to do more; I needed to start something new, or I wouldn't be able to continue in this fight. I need a way to block out this anguish that's stuck in my chest and makes me feel like I'm drowning, in addition to the muscle tension that I haven't managed to get rid of."

"And do you feel like you are achieving it?"

"Much better during the hours that I must put all my attention into this new occupation. When I'm there, I get the impression time passes by faster. When I stay home, the hours grow forever."

"I'm glad you are discovering things to do that can be beneficial. This way, you will continue doing it with the certainty that they're working for you."

"I can't wait to feel good enough to go back to work. I have spent most of my savings on medications. Prozac is pretty expensive here in Peru."

"It's certainly expensive. It comes from the U.S.A. You know, the dollar is more expensive than our currency. I guess it's not that expensive in America."

"I'm running out of money, and I fear I may not be able to continue with the treatment."

"That's not an option. You know you can't stop taking this kind of medicine cold turkey. We have seen your progress. This means the medicine is working. You're very close to seeing the results of the treatment in its full capacity."

"I worry I might lose my job. I don't know how much longer they're going to allow me to be on a leave of absence."

The doctor advised me, "Just a little more patience. Focus first on your health; the rest is secondary. You're going to have to learn to set priorities. If you go on worrying about losing work or running out of money, it could interfere with your recovery.

Money is necessary, I know. There are so many things you can only do if you have money. However, many more things can't be done without health. If you had to choose between losing your job and returning to the dire state you were in several weeks ago, which would you rather happen?"

"If you put it that way, I would prefer anything, no matter how bad, to falling into the flames of hell again. I know that nothing, absolutely nothing, would be worse than reliving this terrifying experience."

"I'm glad you finally understand what your priorities should be."

"I understand. But I guess my anxiety is something I'll have to continue dealing with."

"You'll recover from both your MDD and anxiety. However, as you say, you are anxious by nature. You'll have to learn strategies to tame your anxiety and prevent it from escalating."

"Okay. I'll do whatever it takes. Nonetheless, I wish I were more like my dear friends at work. They are carefree, witty, and relaxed. I've never heard them talk about serious anxiety or stress. They told me they couldn't understand why I was going through all of this. Why, if we were having so much fun at work?"

"I know it's hard for people without your problem to understand those who are different."

"It must be. But you didn't have any trouble understanding me from the very beginning."

Then, unintentionally, I turned intrusive and asked, "Are you also different, doctor?"

Dr. E. just smiled at me. Then, he started talking about something else.

*My Journal – Excerpt 6

"Although many of the symptoms of the disease aren't as intense, I still haven't been able to free myself thoroughly.

The sensation of heaviness I carry on my body isn't as bad, but it's still there. My limbs still feel like they are covered in metal. Will I ever be able to get rid of the fatigue completely?

Nonetheless, I think I am improving because I haven't been crying for quite a while."

*Stress-Driven Neurobiological Illness and ADDICTIONS

According to the National Center for Drug Abuse Statistics:

- 138.543 million or 50 percent of people 12 and older have used illicit drugs at least once, and 25.4 percent of illegal drug users have a drug disorder.

- 138.522 million Americans 12 and over drink alcohol, and 28.320 million or 20.4 percent of them have an alcohol use disorder.

- 57.277 million people use tobacco or nicotine products (vape).

- Drug overdose deaths in the US since 2000 are nearing one million.

- The federal budget for drug control in 2020 was $35 billion.

The National Institute of Drug Abuse refers to addiction as "a chronic, relapsing disorder characterized by compulsive drug seeking and use despite adverse consequences. It is considered a brain disorder because it involves functional changes to brain circuits involved in reward, stress, and self-control. Those changes may last a long time after a person has stopped taking drugs."

It is possible for some people to engage in maladaptive behavior in an attempt to cope with their undiagnosed SDNBI. Some may start drinking alcohol, for example, to ease their anxiety. It's a fact alcohol is a nervous system depressant. Therefore, it would make sense to think these people may be using alcohol to help them relax when they feel stressed, tense, or too nervous to function. Similarly, this may also be true about abusing tobacco or other legal or illegal drugs.

Of course, not everybody gets involved in this kind of behavior for the same reasons. We can't deny some people are irresponsible and of little morality. Criminals do illegal drugs without any remorse just because they enjoy doing it. And more importantly, they don't have any intention of changing their lifestyle.

Here, I'm talking about those kids who used to be well-behaved, responsible, and good students. Sometimes, peer pressure makes them start doing drugs, and because of their underlying SDNBI, they are more likely to develop an addiction.

I'm talking about good fathers and good mothers who were always good examples for their children. There are cases in which they were prescribed painkillers by their physicians, then they got hooked, and their ability to exert self-control became impaired. We need to know that drugs hijack the reward system in the brain, turning the person's natural needs, like food and water, into drug needs. Basically, these people got addicted without their consent.

I'm also talking about anyone who has shown themselves to be hard-working, reliable, and productive human beings in the past. These people can show drastic personality changes to the point where they may turn into someone they don't want to be. They feel ashamed, and they **do want** to change, but for some reason, they can't succeed. There must be an underlying reason since not everybody gets addicted to drugs when they try them.

Addiction may not be the core problem. The main issue could be the reason why they started the behavior in the first place. If they get successful medical treatment and are liberated from their SDNBI, they wouldn't have the need to use these coping mechanisms, and the addiction would be resolved as a consequence.

NINTH WEEK

Eight weeks had passed already. Two months! But I was still in the fight. I was wondering if Dr. E. had been too optimistic and maybe my full recovery was never going to happen.

However, I couldn't deny I had improved enough to perform certain tasks. Having the opportunity to help with my family business was my best self-help tool. Before I got sick, I had always contributed toward paying the expenses of the house. Now, I wasn't able to do so, and I worried a lot about the situation. Knowing I was collaborating with the economy of the house again added meaning to my efforts.

Implementing one more of my self-help techniques, I read books in bed right before sleep. Since it took some time for the sleeping pills to take effect, reading helped me with the process.

One evening, after taking my sleeping pill, I sat in bed, getting ready to read my book. Before I started reading, I felt a weird sensation in my legs. I looked at them, and I felt like rubbing them. They were still sore. I kept caressing them for a few minutes. I closed my eyes and visualized my legs in the same way I was feeling them. I could see them still covered in metal; they still weighed on me. I was still feeling physically tired, too. Reflecting on everything about this long and unpleasant journey, my symptoms, the treatment, all the efforts I had made so far to keep going, some of my improvements, and the issues still waiting to be resolved, I began feeling sleepy. That night, I had a very meaningful dream.

*From a caterpillar to a butterfly

In my dream, I saw myself lying in bed. Again, I felt a weird sensation on my legs. It made me sit up and start caressing them back and forth in a gentle manner, exactly as I had been doing right before falling asleep. While I was looking at myself rubbing my legs, trying to diminish the soreness, to my amazement, I noticed the metal they had been wrapped in for so long started to melt down. Little by little, the metal was separating from my legs. I kept observing the slow process for as long as it took. I couldn't know it was just a dream, so I was astonished by what I was witnessing.

I started feeling lighter. And I was experiencing positive emotions, something I hadn't been able to do since I got sick.

In the distance, I heard a voice calling me, "Evelyn, Evelyn, ... It's time to get up."

It was Mom waking me up for work. When I opened my eyes, I almost felt disappointed that it had been just a dream.

I sat up on my bed. I stayed there, still thinking about how real my dream had felt. I reached for my legs and started caressing them one more time. They weren't sore anymore. I bent my knees back and forth several times. They were flexible. I was ecstatic to see I could bend my knees smoothly. I went on caressing other parts of my body to check if those muscles were still sore. I checked on my arms, my back, my torso, etc. They felt fine.

Immediately after, I set out on a journey into my internal world, wishing it had become as beautiful as the external one. Within my soul, I searched for my anxiety, my anguish, and my sorrow, but I couldn't find them. I called out to my nervousness and my sense of being stressed, but they didn't answer. I felt at peace.

I got up, and I started getting ready for work. I was amazed to see I could get dressed fast and without having to make any effort. I was ready for work in no time! I observed my surroundings. The colors around the house looked fresher and more vibrant. For some reason, I found things more pleasant-looking.

Not only was I feeling overjoyed, but I was also feeling hungry. I hurried to the kitchen and told my mom about what was going on with me, about this sort of homecoming I was experiencing. Mom was delighted to hear the news, and she just loved serving me breakfast!

I kept improving with time. I wasn't feeling the pressure on my chest that used to cut my breath short. Now, I could breathe smoothly.

My body didn't weigh on me anymore. I felt light and strong enough to even go for a run.

Shortly after, I could go back to work. I was feeling fresh and renewed, with brand new batteries, ready to retake my life. My buddies at work rejoiced to see me return. After work, we went out for food and started making early plans for the following weekend.

Dante, my ex-boyfriend, came home to visit. He said he was impressed by the remarkable changes in me. He said I was "me" again. For him, I was somebody else while I was sick. He said he couldn't recognize me in that person. We started going out, and later I accepted to be his girlfriend again.

More improvements came along. Sex didn't feel senseless anymore. It was fun, and I enjoyed it. Two years later, Dante and I decided to get married. On my wedding day, I was as happy as I could be.

~ ~ ~

Dear reader,

If you feel that this book can help someone else, share this information with your friends.

Please leave a review to help more people discover this book and benefit from it.

Thank you.

https://www.amazon.com/Cannot-Dealing-Depression-Anxiety-Thoughts-ebook/dp/B0CCMYQ832/ref=monarch_sidesheets

CHAPTER 6

CONSEQUENCES OF THE WRONG PERCEPTION

BIAS IS MAKING SOME PEOPLE SAY ABSURD THINGS ABOUT SDNBI

Many times, major depression is seen as something common and within our control. I have watched speeches and read books on this matter; many don't match reality at all. This is straightforward evidence that whoever said or wrote such things had no clue they were talking about one of the most pervasive diseases a human being can have.

Below, I have listed some of the opinions and statements about the **stress-driven neurobiological illness** that seemed outrageous to me. See how absurd these same statements would sound if they were talking about other illnesses or conditions. I have substituted these other phrases for the word "depression."

This is what I hear when someone talks about SDNBI out of a lack of knowledge:

1.- "It is not your **terminal illness** that is killing you; it's your negative thinking."

2.- "Cure your **advanced cancer** without chemo, radiation, or any medication."

3.- "Cure **your diabetes** in five minutes."

4.- "**Heart disease** is a very common disorder, just like colds."

5.- "Recovering from **autism** can only come about through a continuous act of will."

6.- "The spiritual solution to your **kidney stones.**"

7.- "**Rheumatoid Arthritis** feels safe and comfortable; I can stay home and do nothing."

8.- "Be grateful for your **unbearable suffering**; it will make you a better person."

9.- "**Antibiotics** don't cure **bacterial pneumonia.** People get better because they believe in medicine. Thus, sugar pills can do the same."

10.- "Fight your illness by working out every single day! Having your **femurs broken** shouldn't be an excuse."

11.- "The best **anti-type-1 diabetes** is **not insulin,** but gratitude."

I once read something else that felt like a punch in the face to me. It said, "If you are going through hell, keep going."

For those who are in the midst of this crippling agony, it would be the equivalent of saying, **"If you are burning alive, keep burning."**

LACK OF PERSONALIZED DIAGNOSES AND TREATMENTS

Ignoring the need for individualized approaches toward SDNBI and other so-called mental illnesses frequently results in inaccurate diagnoses and inappropriate treatments. We could divide the affected people into two groups:

The first group is made up of those who are, indeed, seriously ill and need medical intervention. These people are experiencing serious despair and are suffering deeply. They are given advice like "SNAP OUT OF IT! It is all in your head; go to a party, go on a cruise, misbehave, get drunk," etc.

Some people have dared to say that MDD has nothing to do with our biology. I have heard some go as far as to say, "Major depression isn't even an illness!" It's shocking to hear some people with academic preparation, who should know better, give such uninformed opinions.

Furthermore, there are endless videos of certain individuals offering people with MDD magical solutions. They are crossing the line and invading the medical field when they tell ill people that they don't need medication. They usually call themselves "mind-setting **specialists,** depression and life

coaches, mindfulness **experts,"** etc. I wonder where they got such credentials.

Not knowing that their struggles are mainly physical makes the affected individuals believe that, in fact, they haven't done their best yet. And they continue making the effort to keep going. They keep on dragging themselves through the days, hoping this will pass soon (this is very typical of people who consider themselves fighters, the ones who never give up, and those with high self-esteem, contrary to what is usually said).

Then, weeks, months, and even years pass by, and far from improving, they worsen. For not having received proper information and effective treatment on time, these people keep going for too long until it's too much. As the nervous system is subject to wear and tear, it eventually gets so worn out that it loses its capacity to self-regulate. The affected people are now seriously ill with an advanced stage of the disease. As we can see, people who belong to this group get ill not because they didn't try enough, but because they tried too hard!

The second group of victims is made up of people going through psychological pain, possibly due to traumatic events they suffered in the past or due to current adverse circumstances. All they may need is some advice on how to cope with their life difficulties. They definitely need to feel the love and understanding of family and friends. Sometimes, social intervention is the answer to the problem. Some people may need help finding a new job, finding health care, getting shelter – in the case of victims of domestic violence – or even having access to some financial relief. External difficulties can also cause great distress. Sometimes, these people are told that their emotional struggles are signs of a mental disorder and that they are sick. Consequently, these individuals end up embarking on long, detrimental, expensive, and totally unnecessary treatments that may end up haunting them for a long time. I know this is true because I've been in each of these two groups at different times and under different circumstances.

*My Follow-up Story:

After getting married, Dante and I agreed to dedicate most of our time to working hard so we could save money to buy our first real estate property. Because of this, we also decided we wouldn't have children for the first four years.

A few years later, the honeymoon began to slip away, unfortunately. Dante wasn't focusing on our commitment to obtaining financial stability. For me, it was my priority because I was eager to have children, but I didn't want to bring them into a poor environment where they would lack basic things like I did while growing up. So, I kept reminding him of our initial plans.

A few more years passed, but Dante wasn't showing his disposition to make things work. I felt troubled and disappointed and did not know what else I should do. As time passed and our situation wasn't improving, I finally got the courage to talk about divorce.

Dante wouldn't agree to end our marriage. I tried to leave him several times, but he wouldn't let me go. He kept promising he would change, and I kept giving him one opportunity after another. The stress and anxiety I was going through began to undermine my physical and emotional balance again.

The relationship turned out so bitter, to the point where, in the middle of a heated argument, he pointed a gun at me. This incident was a deal breaker for me. This needed to end. But how could I do it without risking my life? I felt trapped. This was the worst scenario for someone with a latent disease that feeds on stress.

For months and months, I kept thinking about options. If I just moved out and changed jobs, he wouldn't have had any trouble finding me because there weren't many places in the city where I could work as a teacher of English. Eventually, I realized I had no other option but to move abroad.

And so, I did.

Once I had my passport and my plane ticket, I left for the airport, bringing just one suitcase. This was all I had left after ten years of an unhealthy marriage. I boarded my plane feeling devastated. I was leaving behind so many dreams that never came true, especially my ultimate dream of having children.

Then, here I was in America, away from my country, my family, my friends, and my culture, having to start all over again. In the beginning, everything was tough in all aspects. The stress I had accumulated all those years had left its imprint on me already.

The chronic fatigue wouldn't go away. I didn't like the idea of starting medication again, but I knew I needed it.

Within the first two years, things had improved for me. I was working and making enough money to support myself and send some to my mom in Peru. The future was promising, and I was delighted.

Sometime after, something marvelous happened to me. I met a wonderful man! He was a kind soul, a gentleman, a caring human being, and he was even handsome. Soon, we established a beautiful relationship. It seemed I was finally going to have the family of my dreams.

However, fate, destiny, or karma finally imposed its will on me when I needed surgery. They removed my uterus. This event certainly knocked me out in a way I couldn't have ever imagined.

After the hysterectomy, I was constantly assaulted by the raw reality that my most beloved dream of feeling a life growing inside of me would never come true. I began experiencing uncontrollable levels of despair. Anxiety attacks rapidly got bigger and bigger, like a snowball. I was inconsolable, crushed.

I felt the only thing that could ease my pain would be turning back the clock, stepping into the past, getting pregnant, and having my baby without worrying about external circumstances. As I confronted the fact that there was absolutely nothing I could do about it, intense frustration and almost indescribable desperation invaded my whole being.

Feeling overwhelmed, I decided to consult my psychiatrist again. After a few minutes of talking, the doctor handed me a business card. It was a referral to another doctor for specialty treatment. I was half listening while heavy tears rolled down my cheeks. I don't think I even heard what treatment the doctor was prescribing. It lacked any importance to me anyway because I was thinking, "No treatment is going to turn back the clock, and that's all I need."

The doctor hypothesized it was the illness that was causing me to overreact to my loss, and this ECT was going to correct it and make me feel better. I decided to trust the doctor's judgment. After all, doctors know better, I thought.

The first time my husband and I arrived at the hospital for Electro Convulsive Therapy, we had a chance to talk with the doctor in charge of administering the procedure. Dr. Gary told us this practice was safe, I wasn't going to feel a thing, and I could go back home right after without any problem.

After the sixth or seventh treatment session, I still wasn't feeling any better. Soon after that, something unthinkable happened. Something that demonstrated my horror movie had even more horrifying scenes left for me.

I was in my sitting room, talking to my husband about an errand he had planned to run on Thursday. He said something like, "I am going to run this errand tomorrow because I can only do it on a Thursday."

I immediately corrected him and said, "Darling, tomorrow is Tuesday."

"No, it is not. It is Thursday," he insisted.

So, I asked him to hand me a calendar on the refrigerator door. I examined the calendar, and I confirmed I was right; the following day was Tuesday, not Thursday.

I felt so puzzled by my husband's confusion. It was rare for him. He had always been sharp and smart.

He then went silent and looked at me as if he were scared, surprised, and confused at the same time. Next, without any intention to continue arguing, he sat next to me, held my hand, and asked softly, "Don't you remember?"

"Do I remember what?" I asked, almost annoyed.

"Don't you remember you stayed at the hospital for the last few days?"

"What?" I exclaimed in disbelief.

He went on. "After the application of the ECT, you showed an adverse reaction to the treatment. The doctor decided you should remain at the hospital until you become better. You stayed there for five days straight."

I froze! I had no recollection whatsoever of those days. A cascade of intense, disturbing emotions began to invade me from head to toe. So many thoughts started crossing my mind at the speed of light. They were like flashes, picturing the new obstacles I would have to overcome now. This was something way different from any other challenge I had faced in my life, and I sure had had serious ones. This treatment was supposed to make me better, not worse. However, it caused my brain to lose consciousness. "Am I going to be able to continue working in this condition?" It was the first thought that came to my mind. "How am I going to comply with my financial responsibilities if I'm not able to work anymore? OMG, I will turn into a burden for my husband. He's an outstanding human being; he doesn't deserve all the trouble I am bringing into his life. He deserves better." This was the first time ever I felt like I was thoroughly disabled. I felt horrified!

Sometime after, the doctor explained to us that the negative reaction I had experienced wasn't uncommon. He said it happened from time to time. Then, he indicated I needed to continue with the treatment. I needed to finish a whole round of treatment sessions before we could see results. Again, I thought, "Doctors know better." And I went back to the hospital to complete the round of this ECT.

As they continued discharging electricity into my brain, the side effects became more disturbing. My memory was seriously slipping away to the point where I couldn't remember things I had done or what I had eaten just a few hours before. I wasn't even able to call things by their names. I would try and try to bring words to my mind, but no matter how hard I tried, most of the time, it didn't happen.

One day, my husband asked me if I needed something from the grocery store because he was about to go there. I had three things in my mind that I needed. So, I replied, "Yes, can you please get me some, some... I couldn't recall what I was about to say.

All of this was so destabilizing to me. I couldn't hold even a short conversation because, most of the time, I couldn't retrieve the words I needed. Talking over the phone was simply impossible. Furthermore, when my husband asked if I remembered going to such and such a place, I had no clue I had been in those places before. I felt like I was in the twilight zone. (Many other memories around that time I have lost for good).

After they had cooked my brain thirteen times, I finally concluded that this treatment was the opposite of what I had been promised. I was terribly hurt. Eventually, I decided to give Doctor Gary a call. I needed to let him know I wasn't feeling better and the treatment wasn't helping me.

I was expecting some explanation from my doctor. I thought he would sound sympathetic and concerned over the fact that I wasn't finding relief. But that wasn't the case. Over the phone, he said these words, "It may not be helping you, ma'am, but it doesn't mean the treatment doesn't work. I know my treatment does work. Many people have improved a lot with it and…."

While listening to what the doctor was telling me, I felt insulted and so disrespected that I could no longer continue listening. I hung up on him.

What the doctor told me made me think of the following analogy:

Can you imagine saying to the server at a restaurant, "Excuse me, sir, there is an insect in my food," and this person responds in an angry voice, "Don't complain because it's just you who has a problem with the food. All the other customers are satisfied. You should be happy for them. By the way, you need to pay the check anyway because we served the food...."

At present, I can say I know what was going on with me at the time. I was just grieving my loss. Now, I know my emotions were intense because what I had lost meant so much to me. Now, I know I needed emotional support. I needed to talk about everything in my mind that was hurting and go over the thoughts and beliefs down in my soul that were tormenting me. Also, I needed advice from someone who had gone through a similar situation, someone with the ability to pass on the conviction that it was possible to heal after a traumatic experience of this kind because they had done so before. And above all, I needed to learn techniques to deal with my irreparable loss.

It feels so surreal every time I recall being given such an extreme procedure when all I needed was an adjunctive emotional and psychological intervention, especially because I was already on medication. Eventually, if it hadn't been for my decision to stop this barbaric treatment, they would've continued zapping my brain thirteen or so more times.

Through social media, I have learned about many other similarly terrible stories about ECT. Unfortunately, I haven't been the only one.

LACK OF PATIENT-SHIELDING REGULATIONS

Because most of us feel vulnerable when we feel seriously ill, we tend to accept treatments that promise to relieve us from our pain and suffering without much thought, like the treatment I was given by Dr. Gary. Higher health authorities should approve this type of treatment before it is administered. Physicians should present their arguments explaining why they think the patient needs a procedure like this. Let's keep in mind that damage to the brain can result in damage to our cognitive abilities and our whole body.

Also, patients should be given thorough information about the pros and cons of the procedures, verbally and in writing. We need to be given the time to read the documents and analyze the implications before signing any authorization.

Health authorities should also enforce the inclusion of detailed informed consent in the patient's records. Such informed consent should include the following information:

1. Many so-called mental disorders are caused by **undetected,** underlying physical conditions.

2. Antidepressants cure **physical** illness, not the mind.

3. Psychiatric drugs may cause serious side effects. They should be used **only when absolutely necessary.**

4. For mild cases, there are alternative paths that **do not** involve drugs.

5. Emotional/psychological disturbances that cause people to feel depressed (sad) are **not** illnesses.

When it comes to major depressive disorder (MDD), a well-informed patient should be a **collaborator** in the process of diagnosing and deciding what type of treatment suits their needs. The patient's input is crucial for making the right decision. Who can know better than the patient himself/herself about what's going on in his/her life? Only well-informed patients can know if there are any external issues, something specific that may be causing their distress, or if their symptoms are internally generated. The patient, and the patient only, can know if his/her distress is out of control. And if that's the case, their psychiatrist can recommend treatment with drugs or other medical means. Also, the client can know if all he/she needs is talk therapy.

CHAPTER 7

A REVIEW OF MENTAL ILLNESS

WHAT EXACTLY IS MENTAL ILLNESS?

The following are a couple of definitions of mental Illness.

A.- "Mental illnesses are health conditions involving changes in emotion, thinking or behavior (or a combination of these). Mental illnesses are associated with distress and/or problems functioning in social, work, or family activities. Mental illness is nothing to be ashamed of. It is a medical problem, just like heart disease or diabetes."
—American Psychiatric Association.

B.- "Mental illnesses are common in the United States. Nearly one in five U.S. adults live with a mental Illness (52.9 million in 2020). Mental illnesses include many different conditions that vary in degree of severity, ranging from mild to moderate to severe. Two broad categories can be used to describe these conditions: Any Mental Illness (AMI) and Serious Mental Illness (SMI). AMI encompasses all recognized mental illnesses. SMI is a smaller and more severe subset of AMI.

Any Mental Illness

Any mental illness (AMI) is defined as a mental, behavioral, or emotional disorder. AMI can vary in impact, ranging from no impairment to mild, moderate, and even severe impairment (e.g., individuals with serious mental illness as defined below).

Serious Mental Illness

Serious mental illness (SMI) is defined as a mental, behavioral, or emotional disorder resulting in serious functional impairment that substantially interferes with or limits one or more major life activities. The burden of mental illnesses is mainly concentrated among those who experience disability due to SMI."

The data presented here are from the 2020 National Survey on Drug Use and Health (NSDUH) by the Substance Abuse and Mental Health Services Administration (SAMHSA). —National Institute of Mental Health

After reading the above definitions, I still don't understand what exactly they mean by mental illness. I suggest my readers produce their own simple definitions to test their understanding.

It would be great if the so-called mental illness were explained more precisely, like most diseases such as pneumonia, diabetes, or cancer, for example. For this reason, I decided to look in medical dictionaries for the definitions of such illnesses to see how they differ from how mental illness is defined.

TYPE 2 DIABETES

A disease marked by high glucose in the blood and impaired metabolism of carbohydrates, fats, and proteins, caused by the body's inability to respond to insulin, combined with inadequate production of insulin by the pancreas. The disease, which can occur at any age but typically develops in middle-aged and older adults, often begins with no symptoms, is associated with obesity and inactivity, and may be managed depending on the severity with dietary changes, an exercise regimen, and oral or injectable medications. Also called non-insulin-dependent diabetes, non-insulin-dependent diabetes mellitus

Objective methods for diagnosing Diabetes: Blood tests (Fasting blood glucose [FBG], hemoglobin A1c, oral glucose tolerance test)

PNEUMONIA:

A bacterial, viral infection causes lung inflammation, or fungi, in which the air sacs fill with pus and may become solid. Inflammation may affect both lungs (double p.), one lung (single p.), or only certain lobes.

Conclusive methods for diagnosing: Chest x-rays, sputum culture, pleural fluid culture, blood tests, and CT scans.

CANCER

A term for diseases in which abnormal cells divide without control and can invade nearby tissues. Cancer cells can also spread to other parts of the body through the blood and lymph systems. Quantitative methods for diagnosing: Biopsy, lab tests, imaging tests.

In the above definitions of diseases, we can identify clear biomarkers that allow physicians to arrive at conclusive diagnoses. Also, the descriptions given allow us to extract vital information that can then help us answer questions or clear doubts related to such illnesses.

The following are my observations on the above definitions of the diseases presented:

a. The definitions make it very clear that they are organic diseases produced by the physical body.

b. The organ(s) involved with, or parts of the body affected by the disease, are clearly identified (e.g., lungs, pancreas, body cells).

c. The mechanism of the disease is clearly explained. I mean, they tell us what is going wrong inside the body when we have such diseases.

d. Objective tools exist for diagnosing such diseases. Physicians can arrive at conclusions based on concrete physical evidence.

e. There are standards or official treatments that work for most people.

f. Improvement can be measured.

g. It **is not** possible to either fake or intend to deny having an organic disease of this type; evidence speaks for itself.

Now, let's see how much information we can extract from the descriptions of mental illness presented previously:

a. It's not clear if they are just psychological or also physical.
b. They don't tell us which organ(s) is affected or involved in the illness.
c. The mechanism of the illness isn't described. I mean, they are not explaining what's going wrong inside the body when someone has a mental disorder.
d. There are no conclusive methods for diagnosing such illness.
e. There aren't standard or official treatments that work for most people. Treatments start with trial and error.
f. There's no means, other than the patient's self-report, to measure improvement.
g. It may be possible for someone to fake a mental illness, especially when they have a serious motivation for doing so. e.g., to avoid prosecution for a crime (the insanity defense).

To end the era of opinions and speculation, we need an evidence-based model of diagnosing so-called mental illnesses.

IS IT POSSIBLE TO FAKE MENTAL ILLNESS SUCCESSFULLY?

Between 1969 and 1972, David Rosenhan, professor of law and psychology at Stanford University, CA, USA, conducted an experiment to see if clinicians could tell the difference between someone genuinely suffering from a mental disorder and someone who was faking the symptoms. He wanted to find out whether the current system of classifying and diagnosing so-called mental illnesses really had any validity.

Dr. Rosenhan sent nine normal people, including himself, to psychiatric facilities in different parts of the country for evaluation. These pseudo-patients complained of hallucinating and hearing strange voices telling them weird words.

After the evaluation, doctors diagnosed seven of the pseudo-patients with schizophrenia and one with manic-depressive disorder (bipolar). Once admitted to the hospital, they acted completely normal, and the psychologists and nurses had no suspicion that they had faked their symptoms, not even during their two-week-average stay at the hospital.

In a follow-up study at one hospital, the staff was warned that a few pseudo-patients were going to come and try to get admitted, faking a mental condition. Their job was to tell these fake patients apart from the authentic ones.

Out of the 193 patients they evaluated, 41 were turned away because they were believed to be fake, and another 42 were considered suspects. The funny thing is that this time, Dr. Rosenhan had not sent any pseudo-patients at all.

WHERE IN THE BODY IS MENTAL ILLNESS LOCALIZED?

In ancient civilizations, mental disorders were believed to be caused by certain deities. Ancient world physicians attributed spiritual meaning to their patient's delusions or hallucinations. In the Middle Ages, in Europe, they conceptualized mental illness and epilepsy as the result of the diabolical. They also attributed it to the divine, to something magical, or to a higher power they couldn't quite figure out. Also, in the New Testament, people with epilepsy are portrayed as possessed by demons.

Thousands of years ago, they did not have a minimum understanding of the role of the brain in these phenomena. It is understandable that so long ago, as people could not even imagine the central role of the brain in what is currently called mental illness, they attributed these diseases to non-physical aspects. Our contemporary world is supposed to have evolved from ancient beliefs and thinking regarding so-called mental illness. But have we?

The mind is not an independent entity coming from an unknown or mysterious, non-physical place. If we compare the brain with a computer, the physical brain is the hardware, and the mind is the software.

In the last two decades or so, it has been possible to collect abundant data about the brain and the possible causes of mental illness. The development of brain imaging like fMRI (functional magnetic resonance imaging) and SPECT (single photon emission computed tomography) has made it possible for researchers to look at not only the brain's structure but also its functions. These noninvasive imaging techniques have allowed scientists to look at and analyze the CNS (central nervous system) in living people. These techniques are also tools to measure blood flow and identify brain activity changes in comparison with healthy brains.

SO, IS MENTAL ILLNESS "REALLY" MENTAL?

If we look for a list of the human body organs, we will find that the mind isn't listed among them. So, if the mind isn't an organ, it means it doesn't exist in the physical world. Consequently, it can't get ill or catch a disease. It would essentially be like saying, "My dreams got ill."

The first time I read the title of Thomas Szasz's book *The Myth of Mental Illness*, I thought, "This must be one more of those anti-medicine people." But I kept reading, and even though I didn't agree with everything he said, I realized some of his arguments made sense.

In 1961, Dr. Szasz, a professor of psychiatry at the Upstate Medical Center of the State University of New York at the time, wrote the following:

"For those who regard mental symptoms as a sign of brain disease, the concept of mental illness is 'unnecessary and misleading.' For what they mean is that people so labeled suffer from diseases of the brain; and, if that is what they mean, it would seem better for the sake of clarity to say that and not something else."

By now, we know there is plenty of scientific evidence suggesting mental disorders are actual diseases of the brain. For such reasons, the concept of mental illness is already obsolete and still misleading.

Nowadays, psychiatrists should have the ability to look at the brain the same way a cardiologist can see the heart prior to starting treatment. In his book *Change Your Brain, Change Your Life,* Dr. Daniel Amen, a renowned neuropsychiatrist, highlights the fact that psychiatrists are the only medical doctors who don't look at the organ they are treating. And he believes this is an archaic practice. He adds, "How do you know unless you look?"

SOMETHING TO THINK ABOUT

Many of us must have heard these comments: "Mental Illnesses can be as serious as physical illnesses" and "The mind is very powerful."

It sounds like they make sense, right?

Let me tell you, they don't.

　　a.- We know mental illnesses are brain diseases. Therefore, they ARE PHYSICAL illnesses. The nervous system is a physical part of the body. It is like the electrical wiring running all over a house.

b.- Our physical brain generates electrical energy. This energy, together with neurotransmitters, hormones, proteins, blood, and several other organic elements, makes us conscious and able to think. So, the actual product of brain activity is thoughts; hence, we shouldn't be saying,

"The mind is powerful," but rather, "Our thoughts are powerful."

The word "mind" allows all kinds of speculation and incorrect interpretations of neural processes. If the mind were independent and working parallel to our physical brain, it should have the ability to outlive the ceasing of brain activity. But the fact is that in the absence of brain activity, there's also the absence of consciousness.

The "mind" is just a metaphorical way to talk about our thoughts, our memories, and all the non-physical products generated by and stored in our physical brains. Because of this, we should be talking about our brains and thoughts more than our minds.

"...Men ought to know that from the brain, and the brain only, come our delights, pleasures, pains, and sorrows.

Through the brain, we think, feel, see, hear, and distinguish the bad from the good, the pleasant from the unpleasant...

By this same organ, we acquire knowledge and wisdom; and fears and terrors assail us when it is not healthy...."

HIPPOCRATES

On the Sacred Disease

IS THERE SUCH A THING AS PSYCHOLOGICAL ILLNESS?

Long ago, when there was little knowledge about the brain in relation to psychiatric diseases, doctors used the term "psychological illness." Last century, mental illness was believed to be caused by problematic relationships between children and parents. Nowadays, the phrase "psychological illness" is outdated and no longer corresponds to reality.

Unfortunately, there's a lot of literature, documentaries, interviews, and talks where the speakers still don't make any distinction between psychological issues and psychiatric diseases. Again, they keep talking as if they meant the same.

Using the terms psychological illness and psychiatric illness, as well as mental disorder and brain disorder interchangeably is totally misleading, contributing to the lack of clarity and misunderstandings.

We shouldn't lump psychology and psychiatry together because they have different meanings. They are also represented by two different groups of people with different training, and their approaches are substantially different as well. Most importantly, we must always remember that psychiatry belongs in the medical field. Psychology doesn't.

THE EVER-EXPANDING LIST OF MENTAL DISORDERS

Throughout history, people who were labeled mentally ill were those who were incoherent and unstable, those who weren't able to distinguish between what was real from what was not, people without the capacity to reason, people with psychosis (hallucinations, delusions), and people who could represent a threat to themselves or others.

However, for the last few decades, there has been a tendency to broaden the concept of mental illness. It's been pushed so far that now it seems to have no boundaries. Nowadays, grief, social and economic issues, uncommon personalities, and different ways of thinking or behaving are conceptualized as mental illnesses. So, we no longer have serious and tangible problems or complex situations in life that may understandably cause us feelings of emotional distress or instability. Now, it's called mental illness. When did people's problems and difficulties in life become mental illnesses?

While reading the official classification of mental disorders, I spotted a few I considered relevant at this point. Some of the conditions listed don't seem to be "mental." Others sound more like physical diseases, and some others don't even sound like illnesses at all.

If this trend continues, including more and more normal emotions as mental illnesses, we all will end up labeled as "mentally ill" sooner than later (Other people may have different opinions. I am fine with that because these classifications leave plenty of room for disagreements).

1.- Childhood-Onset Fluency Disorder (Stuttering)

2.- Premenstrual Dysphoric Disorder

3.- Specific Phobia (animals, natural environment, fear of blood, injections, and transfusions, fear of injury)

4.- Trichotillomania (hair-pulling disorder)

5.- Disinhibited Social Engagement Disorder

6.- Enuresis

7.- Unspecified Elimination Disorder

8.- Obstructive Sleep Apnea Hypopnea

9.- Nightmare Disorder

10.- Restless Legs Syndrome

11.- Delayed Ejaculation

12.- Erectile Disorder

13.- Female Orgasmic Disorder

14.- Genito-Pelvic Pain/Penetration Disorder

15.- Premature (Early) Ejaculation

16.- Gender Dysphoria

17.- Alcohol Use Disorder

18.- Caffeine Intoxication

19.- Cannabis Use Disorder

20.- Inhalant Use Disorder

21.- Stimulant Use Disorder

22.- Tobacco Use Disorder

23.- Gambling Disorder

24.- Histrionic Personality Disorder

25.- Exhibitionistic Disorder

26.- Transvestic Disorder

27.- Unspecified Mental Disorder

American Psychiatric Association: Diagnostic and Statistical Manual of Mental Disorders, Fifth Edition. Arlington, VA, American Psychiatric Association, 2013.

*[Definition of Enuresis: involuntary urination, especially by children at night].

THE "MENTALLY ILL" LABEL IS DANGEROUSLY POWERFUL

The phrase mentally ill conveys extremely negative connotations, especially for children and teenagers. Labeling them "mental" at an early age is very likely to damage their self-image or self-esteem and cause them feelings of inferiority compared with their peers who are seen as normal. People with a related organic disease (stemming from the brain and nervous system) who have no cognitive issues (can think clearly) shouldn't be labeled mental.

In his famous study, "Being Sane in an Insane Place," Prof. Rosenhan explains that labeling people "mental" is very powerful. It would be like putting a label on them for life since mental illness is seen as something we can never fully recover from.

He also points out that when people who are not diagnosed with mental illness display aberrant behaviors, such behaviors may not be interpreted as signs of psychopathy but just not given much importance, justified, or even ignored. But in the presence of such a diagnosis, these same behaviors are more often attributed to psychopathy. Prof. Rosenhan argued, "This points more to the enormous overlap in behaviors of the sane and the insane than to the competence of psychiatrists, psychologists, or nurses."

*My own experience with the "mentally ill" label

I previously talked about the time when I had issues with my stomach. I would get terrible stomachaches, bad enough that I had to get pain medicine intravenously. Hoping to learn about the root of my problem, I had all kinds of tests run. But the physicians couldn't find the cause of my stomach issues.

Later, I got ill with clinical depression, as you know. Clinical depression (SDNBI) is classified as a mental illness, which would supposedly make me a mentally ill person. Now, I had a strong label stuck to my forehead. From then on, when I had other episodes of intense stomachaches, as soon as doctors at the ER learned about my so-called mental illness, they wouldn't take me seriously. They just gave me a shot for the pain and sent me back home, taking no further action. This situation repeated several times over the next three years.

The day came when the pain and the vomiting wouldn't stop, but the doctors kept giving me pain shots and sending me back home. I felt anxious, stressed out, and fed up!

I needed to handle the situation in a different way to see if I could get a different outcome. This time, I had to pay out of pocket to see a private practice doctor. I warned Mom not to say a word about my depression.

We told this doctor the whole story of my pilgrimage to find out what was wrong with me. After that, he examined me thoroughly and then commented that my abdomen was considerably swollen. He told us he couldn't arrive at a diagnosis at the moment, but he knew there had to be something wrong. He concluded that the only way to find out what was wrong with my stomach was to do exploratory surgery. He was so kind as to write a referral to the ER, letting them know he strongly recommended surgery.

Reluctantly, they agreed to operate on me. But even when I was on the operating table, they still told me I had nothing, and they didn't see the need to perform surgery. But they finally did.

And guess what they found?

I had a birth defect hiding in my intestines. Tiny, folded tissue that was harboring bacteria had been responsible for the pain and vomiting.

When this one quest finally ended, I learned the following: "The fact that they cannot find the root cause of your illness doesn't mean it does not exist."

ENDING THE STIGMA OF MENTAL ILLNESS

I keep hearing in the media and social networks that there are millions of people with mental illness in America who aren't looking for treatment due to the stigma. To help spread the word that mental illness is real, that there are treatments available, and people with this kind of problem should reach out, mental illness organizations and groups of altruistic people are dedicating their time and efforts to campaign against the stigma of mental illness.

Since I usually pay attention to what is said about mental illness and depression, I would say most of the people who aren't looking for treatment are, in reality, having issues of a different nature. They have psychological, emotional, social, and public health issues (e.g., COVID-19 aftermath) and even financial struggles, among many other possible external stressors. When people feel the solution to their problems is beyond their reach due to a lack of resources, for example, anxiety and stress can take over. The feeling of not having any control over their problems can make most people feel trapped and thus emotionally troubled. However, with some personalized assistance, it can be possible for them to succeed in solving their problems and go back to feeling themselves again.

Nonetheless, because nowadays, such issues are considered mental health problems, many people refuse to be labeled "mental." They don't want to identify themselves as such because, in the back of their minds, they don't feel they belong in this category. They are so NOT mentally ill that they can figure this out themselves and don't want to be stigmatized. In this context, we should be using the terms emotional health or psychological health, which is more appropriate and closer to reality than mental health.

In our society, many efforts are being made to try to change our views on mental illness. They usually say mental illness is nothing to be ashamed of, and most people with this type of illness are not violent, so we shouldn't be afraid of them. Nonetheless, it is very confusing when we also see in the literature that the phrase mental illness and the word insanity are used as synonyms. Let's be honest; this is exactly as most societies see them.

If we look up the word insanity, we will find it is a legal term used for defendants who are believed incapable of being responsible for their criminal acts and, so, are found not guilty for reason of insanity. This means the insane can lose contact with reality, and in this state, they can commit crimes without their intention. For that reason, they can't be prosecuted.

The term dementia is commonly seen as a synonym for mental illness, too. People with dementia are believed to have their cognitive abilities compromised (inability to reason, loss of memory,...).

As we can see, prejudice and stigma come from the association between mental illness, insanity, and dementia. So, it's understandable that people try to be cautious when interacting with someone believed to have mental health issues.

If we want to end the stigma, we must eliminate the use of the word "mental." This word is in big part responsible for the stigma because it's not only associated with insanity and dementia but also with craziness. Because of this, people don't look for treatment. They worry about the antecedent that is registered in the health records of a person labeled mentally ill, and they are afraid this may ruin their future careers.

I feel bad for young people with clinical depression who, by the way, are very brave in coming out and talking about their condition because they don't see the danger in identifying themselves as mentally ill.

When I asked for voluntary admission to the psych clinic, I felt so dreadful that I couldn't worry much about the stigma. A couple of days later, when I was feeling less stressed, something happened at that place that made me realize the idea of being associated with mental illness can cause us shame.

"In the morning, after breakfast, some trouble began. Two female patients started an argument. They were fighting over the television. One of them wanted to watch a certain show, but the other wanted to watch a different one. Things were escalating, and they were both loud. So, someone called the nurses who talked to these women when they arrived and tried to find a solution to the conflict.

While this was happening, I saw a group of people standing by a nearby door. They were wearing white gowns and holding books and binders. They looked like doctors, but at the same time, they looked very young. Two more girls joined them. At that moment, I saw something that froze me for a second; then, my whole body switched into fight or flight mode. I felt like my blood pressure was rising, and my face got hot.

One of the last girls that joined the group was an acquaintance. We had friends in common. She happened to be going to school to become a psychologist. It seems they were there to do some practice or something like that. OMG! I felt so embarrassed. Someone was about to recognize me in that place as an inmate. I was thinking about what she would do after seeing me in this place. I was pretty sure she was going to tell some of my friends, and they would tell others, and soon everybody would be saying, 'Evelyn went crazy, and now she is in a mental institution.'

I hid behind a table, and from there, I was half looking out the window. As I saw them approach, my anxiety intensified. I was trying to figure out how I could manage to leave the place before she saw me. I kept looking, and then I saw the whole group stop suddenly and turn around. Somebody had called them. They were being directed to go to a different place. I saw them walk away. What a relief! I felt like I'd been saved by the bell, indeed."

WHEN MIGHT THE MENTALLY ILL LABEL BE APPROPRIATE?

The mental illness diagnosis should be used only for people with brain diseases that include serious cognitive impairment or cognitive disability. However, it would be more appropriate to call the affected people cognitively impaired or cognitively disabled patients.

Cognitive abilities are underlying mental skills that must be in place for us to perceive, comprehend, communicate, and act upon information. Attention, memory, concentration, visual processing, organization and planning, problem-solving, and abstract thinking are other cognitive skills that we need to function in our daily lives.

To help you understand the phrase cognitive disability, I put together a few examples. Let's see how people with this problem fail to interact with others effectively.

Example one:

Person A: Hi, little Johnny. This is Uncle George; can I have a hug?

Person B: (Little Johnny doesn't respond. He does not even turn to look at his uncle and keeps on playing with his toys).

Person A: Johnny, can you hear me?

Person B: (Little Johnny seems not even to be aware of his uncle's presence).

Example two:

Person A: Hi, my name is Rose. How are you doing today?

Person B: Aren't you worried about the aliens coming?

Person A: Aliens?

Person B: There are two in my bedroom already.

Example Three:

Person A: How can I help you, sir?

Person B: (looks at his interlocutor but remains silent).

Person A: Sir, I am asking, how can I help you?

Person B: (doesn't say a word and suddenly punches person A in the face for no reason).

Example Four:

Person A: Ma'am, ma'am, you look troubled. Do you need help?

Person B: Yes, sir. Thank you very much for asking. I need to go back home.

Person A: I can get you a taxi. Where do you live?

Person B: I don't know. I don't remember.

The people labeled "B" in the above examples show signs of problems with their brain mechanisms. The way a healthy brain works is as follows:

- First, the brain takes information from the external (and internal) world through our senses.

- Second, it analyzes the stimulus. The brain sorts it, makes sense of it, and decides upon the right response.

- Third, it executes the right or the most appropriate response.

When any step of the brain mechanism fails, the person will show signs of cognitive impairment or cognitive disability, depending on the seriousness of their condition.

At this step of the book, I want to reinforce my point that there is an urgent need to put boundaries between emotional, psychological, and social issues and physical, organic, and medical diseases. When we aren't aware of the differences, we tend to confuse medical problems with emotional issues and emotional difficulties with medical diseases.

At present, I can say that decades of firsthand subjective experiences, as well as the research I've done and the input of my doctors, allowed me to arrive at the following conclusion:

There are two main kinds of mental illness,

1.- The one that **is not an illness.**

2.- The one that **is**, in fact, **an illness but is not mental.**

"The Only Source of Knowledge is Experience."

Albert Einstein

CHAPTER 8

FINAL REVIEW AND RECOMMENDATIONS

IS THERE A SYSTEM FOR SCREENING SDNBI?

The Patient Health Questionnaire-9 (PHQ-9), a self-report standardized depression rating scale, is commonly used for screening, diagnosing, and monitoring treatment response for major depressive disorder (MDD).

I have created the following screening based on my experience and interviews with other patients with SDNBI. It's not a substitute for medical advice. Talk to your psychiatrist if you need medical treatment.

1. A recent physical examination doesn't show anything abnormal (to rule out other organic causes, complete lab work is advisable. The patient's

medical and psychiatric history, along with the family's, should be assessed).

2. There haven't been radical changes in your life; you haven't had a **recent** loss.

3. There is a history of SDNBI, other so-called mental illnesses, or suicide in the family.

4. Trouble falling asleep, staying asleep, or getting too much sleep.

5. Frequent vivid nightmares from which it's difficult to wake up.

6. Sleep isn't restful.

7. It's hard to get up in the morning because you feel weak and your body feels heavy.

8. Some people may experience sleep paralysis (after waking up, they are unable to move and talk).

9. Loss of appetite or eating uncontrollably, craving carbohydrates.

10. Chronic fatigue*

11. Brain fog

12. Motion sickness

13. Sensitivity to strong smells and high-volume sounds.

14. Anhedonia (the inability to feel pleasure, e.g., eating, playing, having sex, finding comedy funny, etc.).

15. Weak immune system (you catch viral and bacterial infections frequently).

16. Weird allergies or allergies of any kind are common.

17. Recurrent headaches, body aches, or problems with the digestive system.

18. You feel anxious or stressed most of the time, even about good things that are happening to you.

19. Relentless, massive muscle tension that can even cause pain.

20. Serious chest tightness that causes shortness of breath.

21. Lingering symptoms that last several weeks or even months.

22. All your efforts to get better aren't enough. You feel not in control.

23. You may be considering suicide.

*In 1969, Chronic Fatigue Syndrome, or Myalgic Encephalomyelitis, was included in the International Classification of Neurologic Diseases by the World Health Organization.

Recommended YouTube video:

DW DOCUMENTARY – German broadcasters #documentary#dwdocumentary#CFS#chronic fatigue.

FDA-APPROVED MEDICATIONS/TREATMENTS FOR MDD (STRESS-DRIVEN NEUROBIOLOGICAL ILLNESS)

There's no official or standard treatment. All antidepressants (or BRM) are equally effective but differ in side-effect profiles.

Selective Serotonin reuptake inhibitors (SSRIs) include fluoxetine, sertraline, citalopram, escitalopram, paroxetine, and fluvoxamine. They are usually the first line of treatment and the most widely prescribed antidepressants.

Serotonin-norepinephrine reuptake inhibitors (SNRIs) include venlafaxine, duloxetine, desvenlafaxine, levomilnacipran, and milnacipran. They are often used for depressed patients with comorbid pain disorders.

Serotonin modulators are trazodone, vilazodone, and vortioxetine.

Atypical antidepressants include bupropion and mirtazapine. They are often prescribed as monotherapy or as augmenting agents when patients develop sexual side effects due to SSRIs or SNRIs.

Tricyclic antidepressants (TCAs) are amitriptyline, imipramine, nortriptyline, and desipramine.

Monoamine Oxidase inhibitors (MAOIs) available are tranylcypromine, phenelzine, selegiline, and isocarboxazid. MAOIs and TCAs are not commonly used due to the high incidence of side effects and lethality in overdose.

Other medications include mood stabilizers and antipsychotics, which may be added to enhance antidepressant effects.

Transcranial Magnetic Stimulation (TMS) for patients who have failed at least one medical trial.

TMS is a non-invasive therapy that uses targeted magnetic pulses to stimulate areas of the brain that are believed to be underactive in people suffering from major depression.

A small magnetic coil is positioned lightly on your head. As treatment begins, you will hear a clicking sound and feel a tapping sensation on your head. During the treatment session, you remain awake and alert the entire time.

Vagus Nerve Stimulation (VNS) is approved as a long-term adjunctive treatment for treatment-resistant depression for patients who have failed at least four medication trials.

Esketamine nasal spray is to be used in conjunction with an oral antidepressant in treatment-resistant depression for patients who have other antidepressant medications. Also, as-ketamine is a dissociative hallucinogen drug used as a general anesthetic.

Electroconvulsive Therapy (ECT) is used in the following situations:

*Acute suicidality

*Severe depression during pregnancy

*Refusal to eat/drink

*Catatonia

*Severe psychosis

I would like to highlight my gruesome experience with ECT. I would suggest that patients and families do a lot of research about how it really works. You should ask questions like, "What is the mechanism, and in what way exactly am I going to benefit from this treatment? What are the possible side effects? How severe can the side effects be? What is the success rate?" Find out all the answers to these questions, including cost, before deciding on this treatment.

Psychotherapy

*Cognitive-behavioral therapy, Interpersonal, and psychodynamic, among others.

It is crucial to understand that psychotherapy alone is not a medical treatment. Psychotherapy won't do the work for you; it is about helping you to help yourself. The main component for psychotherapy to work is your willingness to let the therapist help you discover your inner world and then modify negative thoughts and inadequate behaviors. You have to get involved in identifying the triggers for your unwellness, creating strategies to cope with life stressors, and becoming emotionally resilient. So, whoever goes to therapy against their will is simply wasting their time and financial resources.

Recommended YouTube videos:

THE TRUTH ABOUT DEPRESSION BBC

The University of Manchester. Full documentary, 2013.

HOW TO END MENTAL ILLNESS

Dr. Daniel Amen, M.D.

Mark Hyman, M.D. Nov. 6/2019.

IMPLEMENTING SELF-HELP TECHNIQUES

Since the central focus in this book is the biological illness SDNBI, I am making the following suggestions, having first in mind the people with the disease. However, those with emotional issues or those who want to gain new insights on this topic can also benefit from the recommendations presented here.

1.- Before you choose any medical treatment, you should have a discussion with your psychiatrist/neuropsychiatrist about your treatment options. You will also need to inquire about the advantages and disadvantages of each option, including possible adverse effects and potential drug interaction. You should ask about the period of time the treatment will take. And, if you don't have health insurance, you should consider costs, too.

2.- In addition, you should talk to your psychiatrist about vitamins and supplements he/she would recommend for you. For example,

- Omega-3 fatty acids are suitable for nerve cell membranes.

- B-12 dietary supplement is for the good functioning of the nervous system.

- B-1 can help with your sleep.

- Vitamin D if you are not getting enough sunlight.

- Vitamin C to reinforce your immune system.

3.- Getting enough sleep is essential. During sleep, the brain does maintenance and recharges for the following day. Herb teas, warm baths, and aromatherapy may help you fall asleep.

4.- Healthy eating is a must. Our nervous system can't recover if we don't provide it with all the nutrients it needs. Junk food, processed food, and too much sugar can prevent healing. You must include healthy fat in your diet. Use olive oil for your salads. For cooking, avocado oil and coconut oil are better. Always remember to drink plenty of water.

5.- If you have the energy to work out or at least go for walks, do it. Working out raises the production of endorphins, the neurotransmitters that can produce feelings of well-being by helping to relax and lower anxiety.

I know this shouldn't be expected from people in advanced stages of the disease because they lack the energy required. Asking them to work out would be like asking someone with broken arms to do the cartwheel.

6.- Make lifestyle changes. If you had a stressful job that could have contributed to your getting sick, you shouldn't go back to the same environment. Find a way to make a living doing what you love.

7.- Toxic interpersonal relationships must be terminated.

8.- Stop watching the news. There is usually unpleasant material that can trigger anxiety.

9.- Read uplifting articles only. Watch shows with no violence.

10.- Start writing a journal as a way to release anxiety and also to track your progress.

11.- Try to focus your attention on things other than yourself. Occupational therapy can help a lot. Spend your time doing things that may interest you and things that don't feel too demanding. For example, reading, writing poems or short stories, book coloring, cooking or baking simple dishes, planting, and doing art like handcrafts, painting, designing, decorating, knitting, embroidering, etc. When you have improved enough, you may be interested in singing lessons, dance lessons, or even learning to play a musical instrument. Learning something new builds new neural connections and contributes to the system of neurogenesis, keeping the brain well-maintained.

12.- Always look for more information regarding SDNBI. Educate yourself on this topic so you can better understand your condition.

13. Learn relaxation techniques. Dedicate some time every day to being alone and meditating.

14.- Get a massage session now and then.

15.- Join a support group, either in person or virtually.

16.- Start socializing- once you feel it would be pleasant to meet new people or reconnect with old friends.

17.- Join a book club or any other group you can identify with. This will give you a sense of community.

18.- If you like helping others, do volunteer work, maybe at church, a school, a senior center, or an animal shelter if you get along with animals better than people.

19.- Be generous and start giving to others who have less than you. Do it privately, without expecting anything in return. Just feel the joy of helping.

20.- Be kind to yourself. Treat yourself as you would treat the person you love the most.

21.- Once you have recovered, you will need to continue taking the medication for a few more months. The withdrawal consists of reducing the dose of the medication little by little.

22.- To prevent relapse, it is advisable to start talk therapy. You must work on keeping your levels of stress and anxiety as low as possible. Don't forget that this disease is sensitive to stress. Stress is the main trigger.

23.- Educating our emotions is an ongoing practice. Slow down; your health must always come first.

24.- Embrace solitude. "He who enjoys his own company is a happy person."

25.- Think of death every day as a way to remind yourself of what is really important in life. When we face death, even our worst troubles or past traumas lose their significance.

CONCLUSION

Depression, anxiety, and mental illness are topics that need extensive revision by medical authorities in relevant fields. The general public needs to hear about the latest data on scientific research and studies showing evidence that most of the so-called mental illnesses actually are brain and nervous system diseases.

It is imperative that we establish a clear demarcation between these bodily ailments and common psychological issues. Addressing two different things as if they meant the same has led to certain people neglecting a life-threatening condition, believing that all they needed was to change their thoughts. Likewise, it has led people with only emotional problems to overreact and start taking medication without the need.

The implementation of a gold standard for treating these brain diseases is fundamental. Mounting evidence suggests that Stress-Driven Neurobiological illness (or MDD) is caused by the interaction of genetics, life adversities, other illnesses, and neurobiological dysfunctions. As long as we continue calling SDNBI "depression," the wrong perception of it being caused by experiential trauma only is never going to change, and the many medical advances needed to save millions of lives aren't going to happen.

It is high time we called things by their names; brain disease and brain health should replace the terms mental illness and mental health. It is also high time psychiatry transitioned to neuro-psychiatry.

If you suspect your problem is more physical than emotional, look for an experienced psychiatrist or neuropsychiatrist, and together, try and find the treatment that can work for you. Brain restorative medications (antidepressants) work by stabilizing the chemical and hormonal levels and reversing damage in certain areas of the brain. Keep in mind that the process of repairing neural connection abnormalities, growing new neurons and forming new networks, making the neural circuits optimal to send and receive electrochemical signals, and eventually having the nervous system repaired requires several weeks to develop and be complete. BRMs do not show immediate results, especially in severe cases. You will need to persevere.

Successful medical treatment will culminate in a rejuvenated brain, renewed neural growth (right in size and number), and more resilient self-regulating circuits. All these positive changes will end the torturous symptoms that SDNBI and anxiety can cause and will finally bring you back to a healthy, meaningful, and peaceful life!

"HEAL YOUR BRAIN AND START LIVING AGAIN."

With love,

Evelyn S. Rodas

~ ~ ~

Dear reader,

More reviews and more recent reviews prompt the algorithms to show this book to more people.

Help me spread the word and save lives; please write a review.

Thank you.

https://www.amazon.com/Cannot-Dealing-Depression-Anxiety-Thoughts-ebook/dp/B0CCMYQ832/ref=monarch_sidesheets

~ ~ ~

Do you have questions?

Would you like to contact me?

Please send me an email at evelynsrodas@post.com

BIBLIOGRAPHY

1. Edmund S. Higgins, Mark S. George. *The Neuroscience of Clinical Psychiatry. The pathophysiology of behavior and mental illness – Third edition.*

2. William Styron. *Darkness Visible. A memoir of madness.*

3. Thomas S. Szasz, M.D. *The Myth of Mental Illness (updated). Foundations of a theory of personal conduct.*

4. Thomas S. Szasz, M.D. *The Myth of Psychotherapy. Mental healing as religion, rhetoric, and repression.*

5. A. Alvarez. *The Savage God. A Study of Suicide.*

6. American Psychiatric Association. *Diagnostic and Statistical Manual of Mental Disorders DSM-5.*

7. Daniel Goleman. *Emotional Intelligence. Why it can matter more than IQ.*

8. Daniel G. Amen, *M.D. Change your brain, change your life (revised and expanded). The breakthrough program for conquering anxiety, depression, obsessiveness, lack of focus, anger, and memory problems.*

9. Kay Redfield Jamison. *Touched with Fire. Manic-depressive illness and the Artistic Temperament.*

10. Harvard Medical School Health Publication. *The brain's impact on depression (2009, 2017).*

11. Harvard Review of Psychiatry: 9/10/2017 – Volume 25 -Issue 5 – p 195-197. *Advances in Psychiatric Research and Practice 25th Anniversary Brief Communication. Neuroimaging in Psychiatry: A Quarter Century of Progress. Silbersweig, David A. M.D.; Rauch, Scott L. M.D.*

12. Johns Hopkins University Medicine Magazine. *New Research into Adolescent Depression (7/14/22).*

13. Yale University certificate course. *Introduction to Psychology (Aug. 2020)*

14. The University of Queensland, Australia, certificate course, *Introduction to Social Psychology (Nov. 2020)*

15. Viktor E. Frankl. *Man's Search for Meaning.*

16. Brooke Shields. *Down Came the Rain.*

17. Steven R. Gundry, M.D. *The Plant Paradox. The hidden dangers in "healthy" foods that cause diseases and weight gain.*

YOUTUBE VIDEOS:

1.- INTEGRATING NEUROSCIENCE INTO 21st CENTURY PSYCHIATRY TRAINING.

UCSF Dept. of Psychiatry and Behavioral Sciences.

David A. Ross, M.D. Ph.D.

June 12, 2018.

2.- THE NEUROBIOLOGY OF DEPRESSION - How Depression Affects the Brain.

Yale Medicine Explains – Yale Medicine.

May 26, 2021.

3.- EXAMINING DEPRESSION THROUGH THE LENS OF THE BRAIN.

Helen Mayberg, M.D.

February 2015.

4.- NEW GENETIC LINK DISCOVERED BETWEEN DEPRESSION AND ANXIETY.

QIMR Berghofer Medical Research Institute.

7NEWS Australia.

2021.

5.- STRESSED – A Documentary Film.

ONE Research Foundation.

2020.

6.- STANFORD'S SAPOLSKY ON DEPRESSION

Full lecture, 2010

7.- TABLETS FOR DEPRESSION – DO ANTIDEPRESSANTS HELP?

DW Documentary.

2023

8.- THE SURPRISINGLY DRAMATIC ROLE OF NUTRITION IN MENTAL HEALTH.

Julia Rucklidge, clinical psychologist.

2014.

9.- THE TRUTH ABOUT DEPRESSION BBC

The University of Manchester. Full documentary.

2013

10.- LIVING WITH DEPRESSION AND ANXIETY.

*Taraji P. Henson: actress, author, activist.

Dec. 3, 2019.

*Kristen Bell, actress and mental health advocate.

2020.

11.- DEEPIKA PADUKONE'S BOUT WITH DEPRESSION.

BRUT India.

05 Oct. 2017.

12.- ATHLETE TO ANOREXIA TO ATHLETE.

Bex's anorexia recovery.

2021.

13.- EATING DISORDERS FROM THE INSIDE OUT.

Laura Hill. Ph.D.

2013.

14.- AN EATING DISORDER TOOK HER LIFE.

Maddie's story.

9NEWS, 2022.

15.- PIPPA MCMANUS: FAMILY NOT WARNED
ABOUT SUICIDE RISK.

ITV News.

2017.

16.- EARLY STRESS LINKED TO EATING
DISORDERS.

ABCN Australia.

2013.

17.- SCIENTISTS INVESTIGATE THE LINK
BETWEEN DEPRESSION AND GUT BACTERIA.

ITV News.

2019.

18.- DO YOU SUFFER FROM ANXIETY OR DEPRESSION?

InHealth: A Washington Hospital Channel.

John A. Engers, M.D. WH Psychiatrist.

2015.

19.- WHAT IS CHRONIC FATIGUE SYNDROME?

The Mysterious Disease that Affects Millions of People Worldwide.

DW Documentary.

Apr.7/2022.

20.- HOW TO END MENTAL ILLNESS.

Dr. Daniel Amen, M.D.

Mark Hyman, M.D.

Nov. 6/2019

21.- WHY DEPRESSION ISN'T ALL IN THE MIND.

Professor Edward Bullmore.

Feel Better Live More podcast

2019.

22.- UNCOVERING THE NEUROBIOLOGY OF DEPRESSION.

Kafui Dzirasa, M.D., PhD.

The Franklin Institute, Philadelphia.

2022.

23.- EL SUICIDIO DE MI HIJO SE PUDO HABER EVITADO (My son's suicide could have been prevented).

Mas Allá del Rosa. Jessica Fernandez.

Feel Better, Live Better podcast.

Nov 7/2018.

24.- I SAW MYSELF AS DEADLY.

Healing after Loss by Suicide

Erica Lennon, licensed psychologist.

2019.

25.- LOSING OR DAUGHTER TO SUICIDE: Kristen and Jeff Durand.

Grateful Living.

2022.

26.- PSEUDOSCIENCE IN MENTAL HEALTH TREATMENTS.

David Tolin, Ph.D., ABPP.

June 11, 2013.

27.- PSYCHIATRY AND BIG PHARMA: EXPOSED.

James Davis, Ph.D.

Nov. 24, 2019.

RESOURCES

1. NATIONAL INSTITUTE OF MENTAL HEALTH - nimh.gov

2. NATIONAL ALLIANCE ON MENTAL ILLNESS - nami.org

3. NATIONAL MENTAL HEALTH ASSOCIATION - nmha.org

4. AMERICAN PSYCHIATRIC ASSOCIATION - psych.org

5. AMERICAN PSYCHOLOGICAL ASSOCIATION - apa.org

6. EUROPEAN PSYCHIATRIC ASSOCIATION – europsy.net

7. WORLD PSYCHIATRIC ASSOCIATION – wpanet.org

8. INTERNATIONAL PSYCHOTHERAPY
   INTEGRATION ASSOCIATION –
   integrativeassociation.com

9. HARVARD MEDICAL SCHOOL HEALTH
   PUBLISHING – health.harvard.edu

10. JOHNS HOPKINS MEDICINE MAGAZINE –
    hopkinsmedicine.org

SUICIDE PREVENTION SITES

1. www.suicidepreventionlifeline.org

2. www.samaritansusa.org

3. www.suicideandmentalhealthassociationinternational.org

4. www.suicidology.org

5. www.spanusa.org

6. www.spiorg.org

7. www.ruokday.com

8. www.thetrevorproject.org

9. www.iasp.info

10. www.suicideinfo.ca

www.ingramcontent.com/pod-product-compliance
Lightning Source LLC
Chambersburg PA
CBHW020442130626
46549CB00001B/256